A CHILD IS BORN

Also by J. Barrie Shepherd

*Praying the Psalms: Daily Meditations
on Cherished Psalms*

*Prayers from the Mount: Daily Meditations
on the Sermon on the Mount*

*Encounters: Poetic Meditations
on the Old Testament*

*A Diary of Prayer: Daily Meditations
on the Parables of Jesus*

Diary of Daily Prayer

13⁰⁰

For Alistair

fellow countryman

colleague in ministry

Barrie

11/95

A CHILD IS BORN

Meditations for Advent and Christmas

J. Barrie Shepherd

The Westminster Press
LOUISVILLE

Scripture quotations are from the Revised Standard Version of the Bible, copyrighted 1946, 1952, © 1971, 1973 by the Division of Christian Education of the National Council of the Churches of Christ in the U.S.A., and are used by permission.

Book design by Christine Schueler

First edition

Published by The Westminster Press®
Louisville, Kentucky 40202

PRINTED IN THE UNITED STATES OF AMERICA
9 8 7 6 5 4 3

Library of Congress Cataloging-in-Publication Data

Shepherd, J. Barrie.
   A child is born : meditations for Advent and Christmas / J. Barrie
Shepherd. — 1st ed.
      p.   cm.
   ISBN 0-664-21410-X

   1. Advent—Meditations. 2. Christmas—Meditations. I. Title.
BV40.S53 1988
242'.33—dc19   87-30978
                                                              CIP

For Dick and Kaye,
Ginny and Jackie too,

who shared with me
the magic
of those earliest Christmases

Contents

Preface

This is now my fifth book using the prayer diary format. As far as I know, this type of devotional book—in which prayers for morning and evening devotions are followed by a space in which the reader/ prayer is encouraged to write his or her own prayers, poems, or other insights—was first devised by the late Principal John Baillie of New College, Edinburgh. In the introduction to my first book, *Diary of Daily Prayer,* I told how I had contrived admission to a graduate- level course on prayer taught by Baillie while I was only a lowly undergraduate at Edinburgh University. Since that first book is now almost fourteen years old, perhaps I might be forgiven for repeating the tale.

I was concealed, as best I could be, high up in the back row of a steeply banked lecture room, between two burly foreign students from America (the same who had smuggled me into the class). When the bell rang to signal the hour, the door opened and a small white- haired figure, almost lost in his shabby teaching robe, shuffled to the podium. As I recall, he had no lecture notes but simply clasped his hands and began to address the class in a voice so resonant and youthful, so filled with life in all its rich abundance, that every person in that room was instantly captivated.

I cannot remember exactly what he told us about prayer. I don't believe I took a single note. But I will never forget the power of his presence, his wisdom, his spiritual integrity. I saw that day the truest, fullest meaning of this experience we call prayer; I was confronted with a life that had been lived out in the presence of the Lord.

People talk to me, and I read sometimes, about a so-called "Scot- tish spirituality." If there be such a thing—and I'm not at all certain about that—but if this phrase has any content, then it refers to an entire way of life, of life lived out in daily conversation with the Giver of all life, with God. This was the life I was privileged to glimpse that day in a chilly Scottish classroom. I thank the Lord again for such a privilege.

This book, if it is to succeed in its purpose, must become your prayer diary, and not only mine. I ask you, urge you, to use its vacant spaces to write down whatever inspiration you might find here and

9

thus let these pages lead you into a fuller exploration of your self, your soul, as found within the holy place of God.

Read and meditate upon the lectionary passages. They are selected from a variety of sources. I have sought at least to include all my favorites, and yours too, I hope. These are texts we know and love because we have heard them, read them, throughout Advent after Advent. They have become a part of our Christmas journey, an essential part of our preparing for that holiest of moments when we kneel before the manger and adore.

As in my other books, I find myself addressing God, at times, as "Father." I realize the problems with that title. I realize I should be able to address God also as "Mother," and I do so on occasion, both in private and public prayer. Yet in these prayers I have tried to share some of the most personal cries of the heart, and at that level I revert to my roots and cry out "Father." I apologize again to all who find this troubling. I invite you freely to substitute the name for God that speaks from your own heart. And I pray that you may, nevertheless, find help and hope within these pages.

I complete this book in the week of my twenty-fifth wedding anniversary and in so doing offer a word of heartfelt thanks to my wife, Mhairi, for many years of patience, sound advice, and loyal support. Thanks also to my four daughters—Alison, Fiona, Nicola, and Catriona—for coping somehow with the additional pressures of a "father who writes prayers." The dedication, however, is to my brothers and sisters, who, in those damp and dreary British winters, many of them in wartime, walked with me first the enchanted way to Bethlehem.

DAY ONE

Isaiah 9:2–7

²The people who walked in darkness
    have seen a great light;
those who dwelt in a land of deep darkness,
    on them has light shined.
³Thou hast multiplied the nation,
    thou hast increased its joy;
they rejoice before thee
    as with joy at the harvest,
    as men rejoice when they divide the spoil.
⁴For the yoke of his burden,
    and the staff for his shoulder,
    the rod of his oppressor,
    thou hast broken as on the day of Midian.
⁵For every boot of the tramping warrior in battle tumult
    and every garment rolled in blood
    will be burned as fuel for the fire.
⁶For to us a child is born,
    to us a son is given;
and the government will be upon his shoulder,
    and his name will be called
"Wonderful Counselor, Mighty God,
    Everlasting Father, Prince of Peace."
⁷Of the increase of his government and of peace
    there will be no end,
upon the throne of David, and over his kingdom,
    to establish it, and to uphold it
with justice and with righteousness
    from this time forth and for evermore.
The zeal of the LORD of hosts will do this.

These Advent promises, Father,
are persistently, insistently communal.
The child is born to *us* for *our* salvation,
and not for "me" or "mine."
They address us as a family, a people, kindred,
commonwealth of peoples, and in so doing
teach us once again that, if we would know
the blessings of this looking-forward season,
if we would ever taste the promised joy
that is to be, then we must shift the focus
of our thinking, acting, even praying,
from the God-almighty self to this communion
in which we stand within your bright creation.

Even the nature of the gift itself,
the gift of a child, defines your promise
in this social way. For a child springs naturally
from the sharing of your love. A child evokes—
demands—cooperation and community. One's life
goes out to meet that of a child and, when
returned, is never quite the same.
And when your people say, or sing together,
"For unto us a child is born . . ."
they are rejoicing in the call to give themselves,
to pour forth gentleness and kindness,
to nurture carefully and mutually
that entrusted tiny glowing spark of life.

In this day, now opening, Lord,
show me the moments and the spaces
where I may fail to see the child, hear its call,
that hand that reaches out toward mine,
that impulse, all too easily discarded, to break through
the deadly isolation of my needs, my hopes, my fears,
and listen to and really hear the problems,
possibilities, of another human life.

As I move across these weeks
toward the manger, Lord, make real for me,
not just your presence as my guide, but also
my companions on the journey. Unite me to the company
of all my fellow pilgrims as we sing,
"For unto us a child is born. . . ."

Amen.

Right at the darkest season of the year,
when the tilting of this spinning earth moves
our northern sphere farthest from the light
and warmth of the sun, we Christians turn
the calendar, Lord, and begin the year again.

Advent we call this season—which means "Coming"—
because in all the busy comings and goings,
over the next few weeks, we will be remembering how
you came among us long ago at Bethlehem and how—
in your good time—you will come again
to bring all to fulfillment.

So, in this drab and darkened world of early winter,
as the nights draw in and we begin to gather
round the hearth, we read of "light in darkness";
we sing of One who is to come; we dream, not just of
this December's gifts, the annual symbols of affection
and of fond regard, but of a future feast when every gift
is opened and revealed to be rejoiced in.

These candles that we light, Lord God,
to mark the weeks that lead us to the manger,
they are for us a lovely, yes, a graceful sign.
Set within a circle made of evergreen, they recall
to us your everlasting covenant, that commitment
to your creatures which, no matter how we wander
from the path, still brings us round—full circle—
to that presence and that peace,
that fundamental knowledge of belonging,
we have sought for all our days, calling it "home."

This candlelight, Father—so fragile,
flickering, vulnerable, yet it speaks to all
with eyes to see of strength that never fails,
of tenderness that cannot be exhausted,
of a golden radiance growing week by week,
and spreading year to year, to light our way
at last within the holiest of holies where
a peasant babe is born to conquer time.

Walk with us through these days,
and guide our pilgrimage toward the manger.

                                        Amen.

DAY TWO

Matthew 25:1–13

¹Then the kingdom of heaven shall be compared to ten maidens who took their lamps and went to meet the bridegroom. ²Five of them were foolish, and five were wise. ³For when the foolish took their lamps, they took no oil with them; ⁴but the wise took flasks of oil with their lamps. ⁵As the bridegroom was delayed, they all slumbered and slept. ⁶But at midnight there was a cry, "Behold, the bridegroom! Come out to meet him." ⁷Then all those maidens rose and trimmed their lamps. ⁸And the foolish said to the wise, "Give us some of your oil, for our lamps are going out." ⁹But the wise replied, "Perhaps there will not be enough for us and for you; go rather to the dealers and buy for yourselves." ¹⁰And while they went to buy, the bridegroom came, and those who were ready went in with him to the marriage feast; and the door was shut. ¹¹Afterward the other maidens came also, saying, "Lord, lord, open to us." ¹²But he replied, "Truly, I say to you, I do not know you." ¹³Watch therefore, for you know neither the day nor the hour.

This story tells me, Lord,
how important it is to be ready;
so much of what I have to do this Advent
is concerned with preparation,
is caught up in all the fuss
of getting ready.

There are the cards, of course,
which should have all been mailed a week ago,
especially the ones for overseas,
likewise the parcels, gift subscriptions,
and the like. Then there are still lots
of presents not yet thought,
let alone bought, ribboned, and gift-wrapped.
How do those people do it, carrying Christmas lists
to all the July sales? I smiled at them last summer
but, envious now, I wish that I had joined them.

On top of all of this,
there is the house to clean and organize,
those festive meals to plan and purchase for,
decorations to be dug out from the basement
or the attic and hung up or set in place
among the evergreens, all kinds of parties
popping up that have to be attended and enjoyed
no matter how I feel. Lord, with all I do
at Advent, do *to* Advent, it's a miracle
I survive, let alone find time
to turn up at the manger.

The wise young women of this story in the gospel
would bid me to get ready in a different way.
The light of their well-filled lamps shines
far beyond these "Shopping Days Till Christmas,"
summons me to prepare my soul,
to trim the dimly burning wick of prayer,
to meditate upon this holy Book,
to perform deeds of genuine love and mercy;
then await with expectation that herald call:
> The bridegroom comes!
> The feast is spread.
> Enter now and dine.
>> Amen.

I always worried, Lord, about the other five,
the foolish ones, I guess,
who got caught with empty lamps
and finally missed the marriage feast
standing in line at the oil dealer's.
What they did or did not do
does not seem all that bad to me.
After all, everyone forgets once in a while.
Their judgment sounds so harsh—
to hear that stern response, "I do not know you."

This parable is one of a long series
of such pictures in which Jesus warns me again
and yet again to watch out, to beware, to be ready.
Whatever your kingdom is, whatever it will be when
it comes, one thing seems sure, it will be unexpected.
More than this, it will leave people out.
Judgment is a reality that cannot be avoided
in any honest reading of these scriptures,
whether I would like it to be there,
believe it should be there, or not.

It is so easy, and so comforting, to get caught up
in pretty manger scenes—gentle Mary, patient Joseph,
silent oxen, and the sweetly sleeping babe—
and then forget the awful bleakness of that stable,
the sheer agony of unprovided birth,
the sudden tramp of marching feet.
Yes, there is a judgment revealed even there,
Lord, at the beginning.

One hope I find in all of this:
that, though I will be judged, my Judge
will be the One who knew that stable birth,
that dreadful cross, that liberated tomb; the One
who healed and taught and embraced children,
fed the hungry, even raised the dead.
So, Lord, tonight I pray for all
who are a little late or come with empty lamps,
including me; that somehow, in your everlasting mercy,
there may be a second sitting, or a spot beside the door
where we can kneel and watch and catch a glimpse,
share a song. In such a hope I lay me down tonight.

Amen.

DAY THREE

❧ ❧

Psalm 90:1–6, 10, 12–14, 17

¹Lord, thou hast been our dwelling place
   in all generations.
²Before the mountains were brought forth,
   or ever thou hadst formed the earth and the world,
   from everlasting to everlasting thou art God.

³Thou turnest man back to the dust,
   and sayest, "Turn back, O children of men!"
⁴For a thousand years in thy sight
   are but as yesterday when it is past,
   or as a watch in the night.

⁵Thou dost sweep men away; they are like a dream,
   like grass which is renewed in the morning:
⁶in the morning it flourishes and is renewed;
   in the evening it fades and withers. . . .

¹⁰The years of our life are threescore and ten,
   or even by reason of strength fourscore;
yet their span is but toil and trouble;
   they are soon gone, and we fly away. . . .
¹²So teach us to number our days
   that we may get a heart of wisdom.

¹³Return, O LORD! How long?
   Have pity on thy servants!
¹⁴Satisfy us in the morning with thy steadfast love,
   that we may rejoice and be glad all our days. . . .
¹⁷Let the favor of the Lord our God be upon us,
   and establish thou the work of our hands upon us,
   yea, the work of our hands establish thou it.

These Advent days, Lord God,
with their long-repeated rituals and customs,
their counting down of weeks and days and hours,
make me acutely conscious of time
and the relentless passage of the years.
It caught me only the other day as I climbed
the attic steps to bring down the decorations
and suddenly thought, Didn't I just put
these things away two or three months ago?
Surely it can't be that time again already!

When I was a child,
Christmas took forever to arrive
and the months stretched out so far
I could scarce remember back one year before.
Nowadays, in this time of a year's dying,
I know too well that momentary glimpse of years,
past Christmases, slipping through my fingers
like sand at the seashore, sifting,
sifting into the empty wind.

This psalm recalls me to
the limits of my days, Lord God,
reminds me that, like grass, I soon will wither,
fade, and be forgotten. Yet, despite all this,
its message cries no morbid, sad self-pity.
Its voice is a majestic one,
singing of a vast divine eternity,
a refuge, dwelling-place secure from everlasting
to everlasting, a God whose purpose and whose wisdom
far outpass the farthest reaches
of my own circumscribed imagination.

Even so this sacred season,
as we wait with expectation for the Child,
as empty hearts prepare him room,
busy lives are charmed to silence, even adoration,
we forget our fearful self-preoccupation
and are drawn within that timeless magic circle
where death becomes irrelevant,
all time becomes the present,
and the present is a gift which
you offer now within this holy birth.
                                        Amen.

Yesterday was the Advent workshop
at the church, Lord, when families—
children, teenagers, senior citizens too—
spent the entire afternoon crafting gifts
or trinkets for the tree, weaving an Advent wreath,
making angels out of straw. Much of the fun,
of course, is making something with the hands;
so many scarcely know the thrill of shaping
something beautiful or functional, that basic pride
and satisfaction at an artifact well turned out.
Even when we fail there is usually someone—
at a church event—who will admire the mess,
encourage us to try again.

The psalmist here, in closing,
turns attention to the blessings found in life
and prays not just for happiness and divine favor,
but that you would "establish the work of our hands."
As I look back, this evening hour, over the day
now ending, I ask myself what there might be
of mine that I could ask you to establish.

So much of what I have done, said, and thought
deserves to perish quite as speedily as possible.
But here and there, perhaps, there have been snatches,
fragments, moments that might possibly endure, I pray.
An impulse, acted on, to make a passing visit
to a friend who I suspect is only just succeeding
in concealing pain. A letter, phone call,
to assist the cause of justice. A gesture, little more,
of human tenderness for one so close whom I have,
too long now, taken for granted.
A check dropped in the mail which will—too easily—
salve my conscience, but also feed a hungry child.
A word of truth spoken in humility and at some cost.
Time set aside for prayer, the private searching
of the secret of your presence, wisdom of your Word.

Lord, as I turn to rest this night,
"establish thou" whatever, of my hands, my heart,
my mind, might be found worthy. Then forgive
the rest through him whose working hands
and heart have fashioned my salvation.

                      Amen.

DAY FOUR
❧ ❧
Romans 13:11–14

[11]Besides this you know what hour it is, how it is full time now for you to wake from sleep. For salvation is nearer to us now than when we first believed; [12]the night is far gone, the day is at hand. Let us then cast off the works of darkness and put on the armor of light; [13]let us conduct ourselves becomingly as in the day, not in reveling and drunkenness, not in debauchery and licentiousness, not in quarreling and jealousy. [14]But put on the Lord Jesus Christ, and make no provision for the flesh, to gratify its desires.

Another morning, Lord, another day.
I wake from sleep, reenter the routine world,
and all too often groan at the grim prospect.
Shower, shave, dress, breakfast, paper, car, work—
the usual—stares back into my newly opened eyes from
behind the bathroom mirror; while that other world,
the world of dreams and fantasy, has fled the moment
I raised head from pillow. Life has trained me
to forget, to shut out those bright and colorful,
bizarre, even frightening escapades,
to ignore whatever import they may bear
and to concentrate instead on daily bread.

This awakening Paul writes of here in Romans is,
in some ways, quite the opposite. It is a call to me
to quit the dreary, gray routine of life-as-usual,
to renounce those daily compromises that reduce
my life to the lowest common level, that make
conformity the be-all and the end-all of my days:
a call to waken to a different kind of living;
a new awareness of the measure of each hour
you give me, Lord; a new appreciation
of the possibilities for richness, wonder,
found within each day; a new vitality that brings
to every moment all the light and texture, yes,
the adventure and enigma which I usually forfeit
when I awaken from my dreams.

To "put on Jesus Christ" should evoke
no dour renunciation of the joy and mystery of life;
it should be an action with much more in it
of vesting oneself in a festal garment,
donning shining armor or bright heraldic robes,
which bring with them a necessary discipline,
but discipline that moves one on a progress
toward triumph, fanfare, exultation.

This awakening you call me to today,
Lord God, is a rising into life, light,
and sunrise, the radiant prospect of eternity.
I hear Paul's rousing cry:
      "The day is at hand."
Now lead me forth to meet it with rejoicing.
                                        Amen.

Going somewhere—
that's what people hope for, Lord:
that this life, this day-to-day existence,
is headed for some kind of worthwhile goal;
a destination, not dead end; a pilgrimage,
rather than some meaningless, tedious exercise
in purposeless prolonged survival.

These four purple weeks of Advent—
their steady measured progression toward
Christmas and its holy consummation—
are a model for the way I would view life.
Yet time—most of the time—is not like that.
It can appear to me to be completely pointless,
the aimless repetition of words, customs,
gestures long since worn down to dust,
a journey that begins before any understanding
has been possible, and ends, all too inevitably
and bleakly, in the dark and spinning void.

In the evening of this, another day,
make clear to me, Lord, the meaning, the purpose,
and the goal of all that has been part and parcel of it.
Help me to allocate its moments, its meetings,
its moods, and its minutiae between
the trivial and the timeless,
the fleeting and the forever; to evaluate
my progress, or my lack thereof,
on this pilgrim way that you have set before me.

Restore to me
that vision set forth so long ago,
the revelation of your goal, your destiny for all,
the realization that all time is moving
to its culmination, to your glorious culmination,
and that I may play my own and necessary part
in that great movement of the ages.

Remind me, Father, of the distance
I have already traveled since I "first believed,"
and hold up before my weary eyes that prize
that shines within the Christmas star:
your gift of my salvation.
Amen.

DAY FIVE
❧ ❧
Isaiah 2:1–5

¹The word which Isaiah the son of Amoz saw concerning Judah and Jerusalem.

> ²It shall come to pass in the latter days
>> that the mountain of the house of the LORD
> shall be established as the highest of the mountains,
>> and shall be raised above the hills;
> and all the nations shall flow to it,
> ³ and many peoples shall come, and say:
> "Come, let us go up to the mountain of the LORD,
>> to the house of the God of Jacob;
> that he may teach us his ways
>> and that we may walk in his paths."
> For out of Zion shall go forth the law,
>> and the word of the LORD from Jerusalem.
> ⁴He shall judge between the nations,
>> and shall decide for many peoples;
> and they shall beat their swords into plowshares,
>> and their spears into pruning hooks;
> nation shall not lift up sword against nation,
>> neither shall they learn war any more.

> ⁵O house of Jacob,
>> come, let us walk
>> in the light of the LORD.

What is it I should look forward to,
Lord God? What is the content of this hope,
the specific definition of this vision of the future
that the texts of Advent hold before me?

Your people, Israel,
held quite definite ideas about the end of time,
ideas which have also shaped the thoughts and dreams
of generations of those who seek to follow Jesus.
Isaiah's vision of the latter days,
his forecast of the future of Mount Zion
as the highest of the mountains,
the one to which all nations shall go up,
has ever since inspired the poets, artists,
prophets, seers, and songwriters.

It is a universal vision, Lord,
despite its seeming focus on Mount Zion.
It depicts a world to come in which all nations,
lands, and peoples worship you as God,
know your laws, seek out your holy ways,
walk in your paths. And ever since that image
first took shape, our hope, my hope,
cannot remain content, confined to any individual
or nation. Hope has to be redrawn with wider boundaries
which will include this whole wide earth.
Salvation demands its own continuing redefinition
until it can embrace this entire human race.
And the destiny of faith is to be shared
with all who seek to name your name
and carry out your will.

As I read the newspapers today
and watch the news, as I encounter
fellow passengers on this graceful
blue-white spaceship we call Earth,
as I form attitudes, pass along opinions,
formulate decisions great or small,
help me, Lord God, to bear in mind the family
you claim me for, keep me loyal to my kith and kin,
yes, every blessed, living, breathing child of yours.
Thus may I start to claim, this very day,
my citizenship in your heavenly kingdom.

                                        Amen.

People who talk about peace, Father,
also tend to talk a great deal about love.
It often seems as if the only solution
they have to offer to the complex problems
of global tensions, ancient rivalries,
the savage competition for dwindling resources,
and indiscriminate, endemic, cruel warfare
is the simplistic belief that if only
everybody would just love everybody,
these age-old riddles would be solved.

Isaiah, at least, is much more realistic.
His portrayal of future shalom,
with those blacksmiths in their smithies
hammering old swords and spears into plowshares,
reshaping on their anvils the instruments of death
into the nurturers of life,
is such a powerful one that people
claim it, sing it, pray it to this day.
Yet the foundations of this revered scene
are laid, not in any vast emotional outpouring of love,
but in law; in fundamental law and justice.

> For out of Zion shall go forth the law,
> and the word of the LORD from Jerusalem.
> He shall judge between the nations,
> and shall decide for many peoples.

Forgive me, Lord, when I claim
to be building peace and all I am doing
is mouthing empty clichés and singing childish songs.
Show me again the role of submission,
willing obedience to your holy law,
of ruthless honesty before its clear demands,
of self-subordination to the higher claim of justice.
Teach me how I can begin, at home,
at work, to forge a lawful, just society,
one where no child of yours need starve
or lack for shelter, family,
basic health care, education.

Make me a peacemaker in truth,
that I might be made ready for the advent
of the Prince of Peace.
                    Amen.

DAY SIX
᭣᭥᭤᭥
Luke 21:25–36

[25]"And there will be signs in sun and moon and stars, and upon the earth distress of nations in perplexity at the roaring of the sea and the waves, [26]men fainting with fear and with foreboding of what is coming on the world; for the powers of the heavens will be shaken. [27]And then they will see the Son of man coming in a cloud with power and great glory. [28]Now when these things begin to take place, look up and raise your heads, because your redemption is drawing near."

[29]And he told them a parable: "Look at the fig tree, and all the trees; [30]as soon as they come out in leaf, you see for yourselves and know that the summer is already near. [31]So also, when you see these things taking place, you know that the kingdom of God is near. [32]Truly, I say to you, this generation will not pass away till all has taken place. [33]Heaven and earth will pass away, but my words will not pass away.

[34]"But take heed to yourselves lest your hearts be weighed down with dissipation and drunkenness and cares of this life, and that day come upon you suddenly like a snare; [35]for it will come upon all who dwell upon the face of the whole earth. [36]But watch at all times, praying that you may have strength to escape all these things that will take place, and to stand before the Son of man."

These words of prophecy, Lord,
have been misunderstood repeatedly.
In epoch after epoch, century after century,
throughout the history of belief and of the church,
scholars, prophets, preachers have proclaimed:
>"The times are ripe.
>The signs are all fulfilled.
>Prepare to meet thy God!"

Again and again Christians have been persuaded
by all this, have put on snow-white robes
and congregated on some lonely mountaintop,
expecting to be swept up into heavenly bliss
at any moment, only to clamber down again
some days later with sheepish looks,
defiant vows to go back to
the scriptures and recalculate.

I find it difficult, Father,
to reconcile this passage, others like it,
with Gospel texts where Jesus said what seems
the very opposite; urging his disciples not to seek
for signs or listen to those who cried "Lo, here!
Lo, there!" or claimed to be Messiah.
If the kingdom truly comes "like a thief in the night,"
then signs like these do not make any sense to me.

On the other hand,
the indications spelled out in this passage
are general enough that they might fit
most times in history, one way or another.
And when I read about
>men fainting with fear and with foreboding
>of what is coming on the world
I feel a shiver of familiarity,
for these words describe too well
this very world that I am living in.

Might it be that your kingdom can be seen,
O God, in any age of great anxiety,
and that redemption truly does draw nigh
to every generation?
Make clear to me, this day,
those signs that point me to your kingdom.

                                   Amen.

> Now when these things begin to take place,
> look up and raise your heads, because
> your redemption is drawing near.

I read these words, Father,
and they recall for me a scene
from Solzhenitsyn's novel *The First Circle*
where Volodin, the promising young Soviet diplomat,
after a long and terror-filled night of "processing"
in the depths of Moscow's dreaded Lubyanka prison,
is taken from his cell,
"his head held high like a bird drinking water,"
with everything suddenly simplified
and absolutely clarified, ready for whatever battles
might lie ahead and filled with a strange
and completely irrational hope.

Does it, perhaps, take times
and trials like those, the brutal shattering
of all the finite, short-term, fleeting hopes
we pin our lives upon most of the time—
hopes for success, for comfort,
for acceptance, eminence, or acclaim—
do we have to be compelled to abandon
all of these before we can fully grasp
the true hope you offer, Lord,
that "redemption" which your Son, my Savior,
proclaims is drawing nigh?

So much of what I wish about
and hope for is petty and trivial.
So many of my sporadic moments of despair
are produced by the destruction of such silly dreams,
the inevitable wrecking of my castles in the air.
In this season when my hope must be renewed,
sift through, with me, the contents
of my hoping, Lord; open my eyes to recognize
the ordinary selfishness that seeks to form
my future entirely on my own behalf.
Then lead me to that hope that never fails,
grows ever stronger as the world about grows darker
and the lights begin to fade: hope in you
and in your Son, who comes to light my darkness,
warm my winter, with his grace.

                Amen.

DAY SEVEN

☙ ❧

Habakkuk 2:1–4

¹I will take my stand to watch,
   and station myself on the tower,
and look forth to see what he will say to me,
   and what I will answer concerning my complaint.
²And the LORD answered me:
"Write the vision;
   make it plain upon tablets,
   so he may run who reads it,
³For still the vision awaits its time;
   it hastens to the end—it will not lie.
If it seem slow, wait for it;
   it will surely come, it will not delay.
⁴Behold, he whose soul is not
   upright in him shall fail,
   but the righteous shall live by his faith."

Habakkuk surely had the right idea
for this hectic world I live in,
this frantic holiday shopping season.
One might almost think he was in advertising,
maybe billboards:

> Make the message plain so folk
> can read it as they rush by.

Yes, for all the wonder,
the theological complexity
of the Christmas story, for all
that is inexplicable, even inexpressible
about the incarnation of your Son,
there is also, at the heart,
a clear, direct word
that can be grasped in an instant,
can be comprehended by even
the most simple of your children, Father.

It can speak, if I permit it,
in the high, street-corner ringing
of a Salvation Army bell. It can grasp
for my attention with all the tender urgency
of a tiny hand that slips snug into mine.
It can demand participation with the pathos
of the "Hundred Neediest Cases" in the newspaper.
It can drive me almost to my knees, bring tears
of joy mixed with regret, through just a whiff
of evergreen, the kindling of a candle.

The message of the angels,
> "Peace on earth . . . good will!"
hardly requires much explanation,
much scholarly research and detailed exposition.
What *is* difficult to understand, Lord,
is how, after all these centuries,
we still cannot, I still cannot,
accept your word and live it.

Forgive my stubborn blindness;
and as I run today guide me to read and then
respond to the message you are sending me
so clearly and so urgently.

> Amen.

What is Martin Luther doing here, Lord?
I mean, this word,
          the just shall live by faith,
is fine for Reformation Sunday—
it shaped the daring concepts
of the great Reformers—but how does it fit
the first week in Advent?

On second thought,
this season overflows with exemplars of faith,
its familiar old stories are populated,
packed with those who lived by trust alone.
There was Mary, after all,
the girl whose confidence in you led her
through public shame and hardship
to perhaps the greatest challenge ever faced
by one of your creation;
Joseph too, whose patient tenderness
and firm reliance on your word gave Mary
the support she so much needed.

I read of Zechariah and Elizabeth,
of their miraculous gift of birth,
and the conviction and the joy with which they gave
their lives, their hopes, into your hands.
Still later there are Simeon and Anna in the temple,
whose staunch belief permitted them to recognize
the child and hail his presentation there
with words of thanks and prophecy.
Sundry shepherds, Wise Men from the East,
and a host of others I can only guess at,
make up the roll of those who at the birth
in Bethlehem had belief enough to see and hear,
respond with courage and determination.

And your call to me these days, Lord God,
is not so much to wallow in nostalgia,
to break out in a sudden rash of generosity
and gift giving, to get all caught up in rituals
with candles, incense, and the like. You invite me
to entrust myself, to place my story within yours,
to set my future firm beside the manger
where your Son may claim it for his own.
                                    Amen.

DAY EIGHT
❦⸱❦
Mark 1:1–8

¹The beginning of the gospel of Jesus Christ, the Son of God.
²As it is written in Isaiah the prophet,
"Behold, I send my messenger before thy face,
who shall prepare thy way;
³the voice of one crying in the wilderness:
Prepare the way of the Lord,
make his paths straight—"
⁴John the baptizer appeared in the wilderness, preaching a baptism of repentance for the forgiveness of sins. ⁵And there went out to him all the country of Judea, and all the people of Jerusalem; and they were baptized by him in the river Jordan, confessing their sins. ⁶Now John was clothed with camel's hair, and had a leather girdle around his waist, and ate locusts and wild honey. ⁷And he preached, saying, "After me comes he who is mightier than I, the thong of whose sandals I am not worthy to stoop down and untie. ⁸I have baptized you with water; but he will baptize you with the Holy Spirit."

In preparing for the coming of your Son,
Lord God, we set aside one Sunday every Advent,
to remember the ministry of John, Jesus' cousin.
What was John's role? How was his mission
different from that of Jesus?

There is an obvious difference in style.
John preached in the wilderness, on the fringes
of his own sophisticated yet corrupt society.
He must have been a colorful individual—
more immediately related to the prophets
of Israel's past—with his odd, unappetizing diet
and his cloak of camel's hair, just like Elijah.
Jesus, on the other hand, moved among the people
where they lived and worked, shared their customs,
meals, style of dress, as far as we can know.

John it was prepared the way,
as Isaiah had foretold it.
Yet no sooner do I learn of him, and sense
his true importance, than he begins to fade away,
to yield place, as he had said he would, to Jesus.

As I prepare, this Advent,
for the coming of the Christ,
there is much to learn from John,
and from his powerful yet humble role.

You teach me, Lord, through John,
the significance of all who point the way:
the vital influence of every quiet witness to the truth,
the often crucial contribution made by those
whose words and lives direct attention past themselves
to One who is the Way, the Truth, the Life.

Forgive me, Father, when my faith becomes
a self-promoting thing, when my testimony speaks
more of my own outstanding virtue and ability
than it does of your great mercy and forgiveness.
Deliver me from all the pompous posturing that lays
its claim so swiftly and so sweetly on my soul.
Let my life this day become a signpost,
an arrow that points clear and true
toward your Son, my Lord.
                              Amen.

Two baptisms I learn of in this passage:
the baptism of John with water,
the baptism of Jesus with the Holy Spirit.
John preached, the gospel tells me,
> a baptism of repentance for
> the forgiveness of sins.

And this repentance would appear to be
the total content of his message, Lord.
It is as if John, preparing the way, led people
to the point of departure from the old life
but had little then to tell about the new.
And since he was a forerunner, one who made straight
the path, this all seems quite consistent.
John's baptism, with water, was an act
of cleansing from the past in which a person
was made ready for the fuller, richer word to come,
the life abundant brought by Christ.

So many churches, preachers, Christians nowadays
seem stuck back in the ministry of John.
They get so caught up in the business of repentance—
all the processes of guilt, confession, contrition,
and the rest—they hardly ever seem to move beyond
into the life in Christ, its glory and its challenge.
Such believers undergo a continuing recurrence
of the fervor and excitement of rebirth.
Yet they lack the steady progress in the faith,
the maturing growth that comes with Christ's
ongoing baptism in the Holy Spirit.

Such a baptism, to me, is more
than any sudden pouring out of raw emotion,
or the gift of strange and unknown tongues.
Rather it is the daily exploration
and appropriation of the gifts of faith, hope, love,
offered freely by the Spirit. It is a lifelong process
by which, in Christ my Lord, my life is opened out,
like his, to your indwelling presence
and to the hurts and needs and crippling fears
of those with whom I share your grace, O God.

Baptize me with your Spirit now. Restore me,
through this night of rest, for service.
> Amen.

DAY NINE

❧ ஃ ❧

Isaiah 40:1–9, 11

¹Comfort, comfort my people, says your God.
²Speak tenderly to Jerusalem,
   and cry to her
that her warfare is ended,
   that her iniquity is pardoned,
that she has received from the LORD's hand
   double for all her sins.

³A voice cries:
"In the wilderness prepare the way of the LORD,
   make straight in the desert a highway for our God.
⁴Every valley shall be lifted up,
   and every mountain and hill be made low;
the uneven ground shall become level,
   and the rough places a plain.
⁵And the glory of the LORD shall be revealed,
   and all flesh shall see it together,
   for the mouth of the LORD has spoken."

⁶A voice says, "Cry!"
   And I said, "What shall I cry?"
All flesh is grass,
   and all its beauty is like the flower of the field.
⁷The grass withers, the flower fades,
   when the breath of the LORD blows upon it;
   surely the people is grass.
⁸The grass withers, the flower fades;
   but the word of our God will stand for ever.

⁹Get you up to a high mountain,
   O Zion, herald of good tidings;
lift up your voice with strength,
   O Jerusalem, herald of good tidings,
   lift it up, fear not;
say to the cities of Judah,
   "Behold your God!" . . .
¹¹He will feed his flock like a shepherd,
   he will gather the lambs in his arms,
he will carry them in his bosom,
   and gently lead those that are with young.

The church has read these words, Lord God,
and found, foreshadowed in them, John the Baptist.
Certainly there is much here that relates
to all he was and said and did.
The mortality of human flesh,
the reality of your forgiveness,
the assurance of a deliverer to come,
these are all of them the Baptist's words
foretold within these verses from Isaiah.

Yet might there be still more than
such a direct prophecy involved here, Father?
Could it be, perhaps, conceivable
that in every human wilderness,
the desert of despair,
the jungle of imprisonment or addiction,
the arctic waste of homelessness and hunger,
the scorching inferno of human hatred, warfare,
prejudice, and all forms of brutality,
a voice is to be heard that cries:
      "Prepare the way of the Lord"?
In the concentration camps of Europe,
where human depravity surely reached its lowest
and its bleakest point, even there the tale is told
of those who rose above the terror and the desolation;
individuals whose faith in you sustained them
through that darkest of all nights
and gave them strength to be
a strength to others.

Is there a way, Lord God, in which
you call on me today to be a John the Baptist?
As I relate to those I meet at work or play,
make me sensitive, aware of all the wilderness
that borders on, even invades, at times,
this civilized world of mine: aware also
of your word, your genuine word of comfort.
So that when I meet a soul lost in the desert
I might be able to "speak tenderly to Jerusalem,"
to communicate by gentle, honest word and deed
the gesture, full of grace, which says:
      "Behold your God!"
                    Amen.

For sheer beauty, Lord,
both in content and in poetry, there are few words
in the scriptures that can equal these.
Read aloud from the pages of the English Bible
they are magnificent. Sung as a tenor aria
in Handel's *Messiah* they resonate within the soul.
Recited in the original Hebrew,
as I heard them first in seminary,
they breathe a passion and a tenderness
that speak direct from heart to listening heart.
If ever human voice might bear the language
of divinity, then Isaiah reached that pinnacle
when he sang these hallowed words.

It is my hope and my belief, my Lord,
that here, as in few other places—until the coming
of the Christ—I can see clear into your heart,
and that heart is filled with love,
with longing for the welfare of your children,
with promise that, however dark the night,
however grim the prospect, your word is sure,
your providence is trustworthy, and you will feed
your flock like a shepherd with his lambs.

Of all the words of Advent,
of warning and of judgment, of preparation
and of admonition to redeem the time,
these words of comfort and the birth of hope,
for me, can set the scene, prepare the way,
make straight a highway for the Christ,
more powerfully, more personally than any others.

Amid the sheer confusion of my overcrowded life,
the failures and futilities, the narrowness
and self-preoccupation, the deadly daily waste
of precious time and talent, I come to you tonight
and in the quietness I hear your voice,
in the solitude I sense your presence,
in this brief moment of eternity—
newborn from time—I know the promise
and the hope and the assurance of good tidings.

Let me rest in this tonight, good Lord.
                              Amen.

DAY TEN
◄§ ፩◄
Luke 3:7–18

[7]He said therefore to the multitudes that came out to be baptized by him, "You brood of vipers! Who warned you to flee from the wrath to come? [8]Bear fruits that befit repentance, and do not begin to say to yourselves, 'We have Abraham as our father'; for I tell you, God is able from these stones to raise up children to Abraham. [9]Even now the axe is laid to the root of the trees; every tree therefore that does not bear good fruit is cut down and thrown into the fire."

[10]And the multitudes asked him, "What then shall we do?" [11]And he answered them, "He who has two coats, let him share with him who has none; and he who has food, let him do likewise." [12]Tax collectors also came to be baptized, and said to him, "Teacher, what shall we do?" [13]And he said to them, "Collect no more than is appointed you." [14]Soldiers also asked him, "And we, what shall we do?" And he said to them, "Rob no one by violence or by false accusation, and be content with your wages."

[15]As the people were in expectation, and all men questioned in their hearts concerning John, whether perhaps he were the Christ, [16]John answered them all, "I baptize you with water; but he who is mightier than I is coming, the thong of whose sandals I am not worthy to untie; he will baptize you with the Holy Spirit and with fire. [17]His winnowing fork is in his hand, to clear his threshing floor, and to gather the wheat into his granary, but the chaff he will burn with unquenchable fire."

[18]So, with many other exhortations, he preached good news to the people.

Luke, the Gospel writer, calls this word
that John the Baptist preached "good news."
     So, with many other exhortations,
     he preached good news to the people.
Yet, when I read his words, Lord,
at least as Luke records them here,
calling the people a "brood of vipers,"
threatening them with wrath and fire to come,
the news does not sound "good" to me.

Is it right to frighten people, God,
to stampede them to your mercy like a herd
of frightened cattle? So many preachers,
down the centuries, have used this same technique,
have portrayed their congregations dangling by
a spider thread above the flames of hell.
So many persons seem to have embraced the faith
in order to evade eternal punishment,
rather than to enter joyful into life abundant.

I question this, Father. How can one choose
to live a selfless life for selfish reasons?
How can I freely love a God who threatens to destroy me
and all that I hold dear? What is the proper role
of fear in the gospel of your grace, Lord God?

Sin is a fearful thing.
Evil is no childish fairy tale,
but a real-life horror story, as the news headlines
make clear every day. This evil may seem far beyond
my own small failings and omissions,
yet the roots are here within. I know them
in myself, when I am honest with myself.
Could it follow therefore that,
before I hear the good news of your grace,
I have to face the bad news of my failures,
with all their fearful consequences?
Might it be that fear, not fear of hell so much
as fear of hell on earth I am creating here and now,
might this fear be the blade that opens up my life,
prepares it for your gospel? If so, then may this day
be fearful, and thus open to your grace.
                          Amen.

Such a universal question, Lord.
A question asked of Jesus, Paul, and Peter
and of preachers, teachers, thinkers ever since.
"If this be true, what can we do about it?"

John the Baptist doesn't mince words here.
He does not go on to ponder, as the gurus might,
the difference between "doing" and "being."
This Baptist preacher does not propose that it's not
what you do, but who, or what you believe,
that really counts. Instead, he gives the people
practical, down-to-earth advice. He looks with them
at their lives, their own particular circumstances,
and spells out just what his gospel,
his "good news," might require of them.

"Share what you have with those who are less fortunate.
Avoid dishonesty, deception, selfish greed in daily work.
Do not abuse whatever power you are charged with
through acts of violence or falsehood. Be content
with what you have, not always seeking after more."

Sensible, reasonable ethics, surely!
A set of standards that should appeal to everyone;
in no way fanatical, radical, or extreme.
Far more moderate, really, than the teachings of the One
who was to follow, your Son, my Savior, Jesus Christ.

Yet even this gospel of John convicts me, Father.
Even these moderate, justifiable standards go far beyond
the measure of *my* customary rule. I share so little
in comparison with all those bare essentials
I persuade myself I need to keep. Dishonesty and deception
have learned to be so subtle in my mind I no longer
easily recognize their soft, seductive voices,
while contentment with my lot seems irresponsible in
a society that survives on rising expectations.

Let these clear words of John bring truth to bear
upon my daily walk, Lord God. Deliver me from foolishness,
all my frantic striving after empty goals.
And lead me in the everlasting way,
through Christ, my Lord.
                    Amen.

DAY ELEVEN
⋖⋗
Psalm 130

¹Out of the depths I cry to thee, O LORD!
² Lord, hear my voice!
Let thy ears be attentive
    to the voice of my supplications!

³If thou, O LORD, shouldst mark iniquities,
    Lord, who could stand?
⁴But there is forgiveness with thee,
    that thou mayest be feared.

⁵I wait for the LORD, my soul waits,
    and in his word I hope;
⁶my soul waits for the LORD
    more than watchmen for the morning,
    more than watchmen for the morning.

⁷O Israel, hope in the LORD!
    For with the LORD there is steadfast love,
    and with him is plenteous redemption.
⁸And he will redeem Israel
    from all his iniquities.

This season is a time of bleakness
and despair for many of your children, Lord.
They hear the melodies of peace and joy,
read about the gestures of goodwill that permeate
these days, glimpse from afar the glowing firesides,
the festive family tables, and know nothing
of this in their own drab lives.
Alone, abandoned, orphaned children
gazing through the bright-lit toy-shop window:
such persons know the depths from which
this psalmist cries to you.

Yet, for all my careful preparation,
my planning for a tasteful and traditional
celebration of the Bethlehem birth, it strikes me
that these others, these people who still find no room
to lay their heads this Christmastide, are closer
to the meaning of it all than I can ever be.
Your son was of their number, after all,
his travel-weary parents found no friendly welcome
waiting when they reached their destination.
For all their deep and genuine faith,
they must have drawn close to despair at times,
must have cried to you, Lord God, out of the depths.

As I prepare myself this day
for your nativity, O God, grant me courage
to look for your Son in the place he is most likely
to be found. Lead me down into the depths
of human hurt and misery and lostness,
there to offer up no easy comfort,
nor even a small check for conscience' sake,
but to listen and to learn, to share
in some small way the depths that they,
and you, have known, endured on my behalf.

Then hear my cry—out of the depths—
my honest, needy call for your forgiveness,
your deliverance, your grace. And send to me
your newborn Son to share my burden, heal my wound,
to join my loneliness and take away my pain.
Thus may I plumb the depths and touch
the sacred height of Christmas.

Amen.

Another year is drawing to a close, Father.
Twelve more months, fifty-two weeks to be set aside,
tied with a faded ribbon, then stored away
in the lumber room of memory and regret.
There is, of course, Christmas coming up,
with its bright festive moments, feasts and parties,
specials on TV, but then the dark sets in again,
old December reasserts its gloomy grasp,
and New Year's Eve recalls the passing year,
the dwindling light, the fleeting time,
the longest chill that lies ahead.

This darkening winter's night
I read the psalmist's words "Out of the depths"
and catch something of the urgency, the fervor of his cry:
     "Lord, hear my voice!
     Let thy ears be attentive
     to the voice of my supplications!"
For without your listening ear, the firm assurance that
"there is forgiveness with you," there is little left
to cling to in all the frantic, artificial joviality
that surrounds the dying of another year.

I can see those weary watchmen
on the loftiest turrets of the city,
pacing the walls and parapets, yawning,
stretching, peering far into the eastern sky
where the horizon lies, yearning for the first
faint signs of light, doubting, almost persuaded
that night will never end, that dawn and sunrise are
mere phantoms of their tired, fevered minds.
And then the cry: "O Israel, hope in the Lord!"

Take all the longing of my life thus far,
Lord God, the prizes never won, the friends
who never realized what they might mean to me,
achievement turned to clay as it was grasped, the love
that ever reaches out and then falls short, again, again . . .
and set it on the battlements of life,
direct its gaze toward the flush of dawn,
and teach my heart to place its hope in you
and in your steadfast love. Then lift me
from the depths into the sunrise.
               Amen.

DAY TWELVE
⋘ ⋙
Romans 15:4–13

⁴For whatever was written in former days was written for our instruction, that by steadfastness and by the encouragement of the scriptures we might have hope. ⁵May the God of steadfastness and encouragement grant you to live in such harmony with one another, in accord with Christ Jesus, ⁶that together you may with one voice glorify the God and Father of our Lord Jesus Christ.

⁷Welcome one another, therefore, as Christ has welcomed you, for the glory of God. ⁸For I tell you that Christ became a servant to the circumcised to show God's truthfulness, in order to confirm the promises given to the patriarchs, ⁹and in order that the Gentiles might glorify God for his mercy. As it is written,

"Therefore I will praise thee among the Gentiles,
and sing to thy name";
¹⁰and again it is said,
"Rejoice, O Gentiles, with his people";
¹¹and again,
"Praise the Lord, all Gentiles,
and let all the peoples praise him";
¹²and further Isaiah says,
"The root of Jesse shall come,
he who rises to rule the Gentiles;
in him shall the Gentiles hope."
¹³May the God of hope fill you with all joy and peace in believing, so that by the power of the Holy Spirit you may abound in hope.

What glowing, cozy scenes this warm word
"welcome" conjures up! A holly wreath hung
on an open door, framing a candle-lighted room,
a crackling log fire. A family arriving, stamping
snow from boots, unwinding scarves, hats, gloves with
fumbling, fond embraces as parents greet children,
grandparents enfold and fondle little bundles
of excitement. Bright packages are then disclosed
and placed around the shining tree. Hot, tingling drinks
soon warm the blood as all are gathered round the hearth
and welcomed home. Yes, Father, home for Christmas.
A precious scene. A phrase filled with magic—
for this season is for welcoming.

Yet how to reconcile this scene, this lovely image
in my mind, with the reality I learn of in the Gospels:
the fact—the shocking, naked fact—that there was
no such welcome for your Son, no room for him,
no cozy fireside, not even space to rest his
newborn head, except a feed box in a barn?

What does it mean, this stark, ironic contrast?
How should I welcome Christmas in a world
where folk still wander without shelter, without food,
where sisters, brothers, know oppression and injustice?
How do I reconcile my own somewhat splendid celebration
with John's word that says:
          "He came unto his own,
            and his own received him not"?
There is still no lack of people who need welcoming.
The means to do so, in a manner finer far
than anything the innkeeper of Bethlehem might offer,
are certainly at my disposal.
Your Son told once about a feast
to which the host sent out and gathered
people from the highways and street corners.
This day, Lord, help me plan to open out my holiday,
my holy day, to the stranger, the unwanted, the alone.
Show me how to make my church not just a decorated
showplace but a refuge, a true sanctuary
where your Child might find a welcome.
Lord, open up my soul and enter in.
                              Amen.

This season is supremely about hope.
It begins as little children, Father, when hope
is pretty much confined to secret tempting packages
concealed about the house. Even as an adult, I fear,
I haven't progressed much beyond that stage.
But hopes do mature as years go by.

I ask myself tonight, What do I truly hope for?
If all the limitations were removed, what would I wish
to find beneath that tree? I guess my first thoughts
run to more, much more, of what I have already:
a winning ticket in the lottery,
new car, new house, new clothes, new everything.
But beyond things, what is it that I really want?
What do I lack and yearn for, deep beneath these toys
and gadgets, novel ways to pass the time?

Might it be life I seek? Oh, not this mere existence
I pursue from day to day, but a different kind of living,
without crippling worry and fear: living that is full,
fulfilled and free, that knows love—love given,
love returned—living no longer haunted as the years
slip away by that grim presence in the shadows that brings
an end to all my lesser hopes. It is life, Lord God,
abundant life, I reach for, struggle for, die for—
yes, hope for as I move across this holy season.

But life was what you gave, on that night
so long ago. That is what it meant when, instead
of all the other things I would have asked for—power,
influence, wealth, knowledge—you sent to us a child.
When you revealed yourself completely, Lord,
not in the whirlwind, earthquake, fire,
not seated on some vast majestic throne,
but lying in a feed box, crying for mother's milk,
you were telling us, telling me, that in this new beginning
there lies all the hope and promise, all the possibility
that I can ever ask, or need, or wish for.

The God of hope, Paul names you.
Then let this hope surround my sleep tonight,
sustain all that I am and wish for
through these Advent days.
                    Amen.

DAY THIRTEEN
⋖§ §⋗
Isaiah 11:1–10

¹There shall come forth a shoot from the stump of Jesse,
  and a branch shall grow out of his roots.
²And the Spirit of the LORD shall rest upon him,
  the spirit of wisdom and understanding,
  the spirit of counsel and might,
  the spirit of knowledge and the fear of the LORD.
³And his delight shall be in the fear of the LORD.

He shall not judge by what his eyes see,
  or decide by what his ears hear;
⁴but with righteousness he shall judge the poor,
  and decide with equity for the meek of the earth;
and he shall smite the earth with the rod of his mouth,
  and with the breath of his lips he shall slay the wicked.
⁵Righteousness shall be the girdle of his waist,
  and faithfulness the girdle of his loins.

⁶The wolf shall dwell with the lamb,
  and the leopard shall lie down with the kid,
and the calf and the lion and the fatling together,
  and a little child shall lead them.
⁷The cow and the bear shall feed;
  their young shall lie down together;
  and the lion shall eat straw like the ox.
⁸The sucking child shall play over the hole of the asp,
  and the weaned child shall put his hand on the adder's den.
⁹They shall not hurt or destroy
  in all my holy mountain;
for the earth shall be full of the knowledge of the LORD
  as the waters cover the sea.

¹⁰In that day the root of Jesse shall stand as an ensign to the peoples; him shall the nations seek, and his dwellings shall be glorious.

Roots are such important things
to us, your wandering children, Lord.
We love to search the records of the past,
to discover where we came from, who we came from.
People proudly trace their ancestry to some
illustrious forebear—there always seems to be one,
at least for those who do all the talking!

Isaiah here, in looking to the future,
also turns toward the past. He views the hope
of Israel to be, to some extent, the true renewal
of what has been and was lost. So that, although
the line of David, Jesse's son, is now in disarray,
if not disgrace, that house will be restored,
made even more illustrious than before.

It seems good to me, Father, that we look back
before looking forward, that our remembering plays
such a major part in preparation for the future.
I can remember, at this time of year, so many Christmases:
under wartime bombing as a child, far from home
on military service, beginning our own home
with our first child. Such memories
are rich and fondly cherished.

Yet more than mere nostalgia is involved.
As I look back I find myself again, I rediscover
who I am in a much broader, fuller view
than in the fleeting glimpse of any given moment.
When I look back I find those I belong with:
family members, friends, enemies as well, many of whom
had almost been forgotten yet have been, still are,
a fundamental part of my identity.

When I look back I find your hand, my God,
tracing in the present and the future from the past,
guiding, prodding at times, comforting, sustaining,
lifting me out of the dust of failure and defeat,
brushing me off, setting me on my feet, back on the road;
and beckoning me onward to the promise
that has brought me safe thus far.

So let me in this day learn from the past
to stride with confidence into your future.

                                        Amen.

What is this "knowledge of the Lord"
which Isaiah claims will someday fill the world
just as the waters cover the sea? I suspect that
he means more than simply knowing all your titles,
Lord, the many names, descriptions, definitions
I can seek out in the scriptures, the creeds
and doctrines of the church.

Knowledge of you, as Isaiah sees it,
O God, is not at all the type of knowing
that we understand today. It must include,
for one example, knowing not just who you are,
but also who I am, whose I am, where I belong in
the great scheme of things, and whom I belong with.
The scene this prophet paints to show
the kind of world such knowledge brings about
makes this clear right away.

For the wolf to lie down with the lamb,
the leopard with the kid, and a little child
to lead them would take more, right now, than all
the stockpiled knowledge gathered since the dawn of time.
This charming vision of the peaceable kingdom
has inspired artists, poets, musicians, and peacemakers
since Isaiah first proclaimed it, but it has been
more of a wistful longing, a sweet "if only" dream,
than a hard firm reality that, here and now,
might be attempted and achieved.

It is not a complex theory.
No complicated plan is here for "peace in our time."
Isaiah simply comprehends that when we know you fully—
as we believe we do in Jesus Christ—then we realize
that any kind of violence is alien to your nature
and our own; then we will see that we were made
for one another and that your greatest gift
and blessing to each one of us is made up
of all the persons, other living beings,
with whom we share the life of your creation.

I thank you for this vision, Lord,
and for the little Child who came, who comes,
to lead this whole creation toward peace.

         Amen.

DAY FOURTEEN
❧ ❧
Revelation 1:4–8

⁴John to the seven churches that are in Asia:

Grace to you and peace from him who is and who was and who is to come, and from the seven spirits who are before his throne, ⁵and from Jesus Christ the faithful witness, the firstborn of the dead, and the ruler of kings on earth.

To him who loves us and has freed us from our sins by his blood ⁶and made us a kingdom, priests to his God and Father, to him be glory and dominion for ever and ever. Amen. ⁷Behold, he is coming with the clouds, and every eye will see him, every one who pierced him; and all tribes of the earth will wail on account of him. Even so. Amen.

⁸"I am the Alpha and the Omega," says the Lord God, who is and who was and who is to come, the Almighty.

What a strange book this is, Father,
and what a stormy and disputed history
it has known in the life of the church.
It is called "The Revelation,"
and yet its message is so cloaked,
concealed in mystery, in bizarre signs and symbols,
in numbers, visions, beasts, demons, and angels,
that this title seems an ironic misnomer.

There have been those, however,
many of them through the centuries,
who have claimed to know the secret that unlocks
the hidden wisdom of this book. Time and again
preachers have drawn parallels from the events
foreseen within these colorful, obscure pages
to their own particular time and circumstance.
By the adding up of numbers, or identifying names
and nations, they have announced their firm conviction
that all is about to be fulfilled. Fortunately
or unfortunately, Lord, not one of them
has yet proved to be right.

The man who wrote this book was a prisoner,
a slave laborer, perhaps, in the Roman camps
on the small island of Patmos. In a time
of fierce persecution, he wrote to encourage
fellow Christians to stand fast by telling them
a vision he had seen of what was soon to come about.
What he saw was not the far-off distant future
but the cosmic struggle going on right then,
a struggle in which the Lamb of God
already claimed the victory.

As I look to the future in this looking-forward season,
deliver me, Lord God, from foolish speculation.
Let me heed the warning of your Son to those who cry,
"Look here! Look there!" Reveal to me that vision
of your Living Word in action in this broken,
yearning world this very day. Then let me join
my strength, my wisdom, and my prayers
to the preparing of your kingdom here and now,
through him who has come, will come,
does come for the saving of your people.
                                        Amen.

People enjoy this phrase,
"the Alpha and Omega," Lord.
Teachers, preachers, theologians,
even ordinary Christians like the sound of it,
feel that, as a title, it has dignity, profundity,
a certain touch of the exotic and arcane.

My problem with it is
that it cuts out the part I live in.
Yes, I agree that you are Alpha—the Beginning.
I affirm with John the Evangelist that,
before anything was, you were;
that all that is has come about through you.
Just as firmly I believe you are Omega, the goal
to whom my life and all creation moves,
that One who will be when all else
has ceased to be.

But what about all that lies in between?
Surely you would not only claim the Prelude
and the Postlude, Father. And so the writer
of this elegant title hastens to expand, to clarify,
as he moves on to speak of you as
        the Lord God, who is and who was
        and who is to come, the Almighty.
Christians spend so much time on the beginning
and the end. They argue endlessly about just when
and how you made this earth, and just as tiresomely
about the eventual bringing of it all to a full stop.
While, in the meantime, you are busy acting now,
creating, even in this very moment, life and hope,
purpose and possibility to be seized upon, believed in,
and lived out. Why do we believe that, like a clockmaker,
you wound the new world up, set the alarm to go off
at the end, and then went about some other business?

At the end of this, another day,
remind me, Father, you were there with me
at the beginning. But recall me also to your guiding
presence every step along the way. Now as I draw
the curtains of my soul, be with me from this end
unto an ever-new beginning.
                    Amen.

DAY FIFTEEN
❧ ❧
Hosea 14:5–9

⁵I will be as the dew to Israel;
   he shall blossom as the lily,
   he shall strike root as the poplar;
⁶his shoots shall spread out;
   his beauty shall be like the olive,
   and his fragrance like Lebanon.
⁷They shall return and dwell beneath my shadow,
   they shall flourish as a garden;
they shall blossom as the vine,
   their fragrance shall be like the wine of Lebanon.

⁸O Ephraim, what have I to do with idols?
   It is I who answer and look after you.
I am like an evergreen cypress,
   from me comes your fruit.

⁹Whoever is wise, let him understand these things;
   whoever is discerning, let him know them;
for the ways of the LORD are right,
   and the upright walk in them,
   but transgressors stumble in them.

This image of Hosea's seems,
at first, quite out of place.
I do not think too much of gardens
in the chill darkness of December, Father.

Of course I should remember there are millions
of fellow Christians who celebrate the birthday
of your Son in summer's heat. Snow and robins,
sleighs and holly berries, despite their traditional
and sentimental charm, have no essential role
to play within this holy season.
Whatever, there is something deeply satisfying
in this scene Hosea paints for me of promised hope.

A garden at the end, as there was at the beginning!
Might this express the longing of a desert folk,
a nomad people who believed their God had saved them
from the wilderness and given them their greatest gift,
the gift of land to till and cultivate and harvest?
Certainly these holy books of Israel are filled
with images of plants and shrubs and flowers,
fields and folds, olive trees and vineyards.

But it is not only Israel
that loves to plant and help things grow.
This is a much more basic human impulse,
one that I and many friends rejoice to share.
In fact, soon after Christmas, the mails will brim
with brightly colored catalogs of seeds and plants,
all springtime's wonder, and people will start dreaming,
scheming, plotting out that fertile sun-blessed spot
where they can play their own creative part
in your miracle of life reborn.

I believe this is a good
and generous impulse in us, Father.
Might it even give expression to a longing
for that other graceful garden lost so long ago?
Might it point toward a yearning for that day
when you will come to us like summer's dew
upon the thirsty grass and bless our souls with
the cool fresh touch of life and growth
that yields abundant harvest?
                              Amen.

Of all of Israel's prophets
with their poetry, their vivid images
and metaphors, I have always found Hosea, Lord,
to be uniquely sympathetic, both passionate
and lyrical, an inspired weaver of your Word.

It is Hosea who most powerfully portrays you
in the terms, relationships, anxieties, and elations
of the human family. He can express your bitter anguish
over Israel in the tormented angry yearning of one
whose marriage is repeatedly betrayed,
yet cannot cease from loving.

Hosea ventures into all the hurt, the tension,
trampled feelings, torn emotions of a parent and a child,
tracing rebellion, rejection, then compassion and forgiveness
as he tells the tale of teenage Israel tearing away from
all the bonds of tenderness, affection, loving-kindness,
patient nurture, then your desperate cry—
> How can I give you up. . . .
> My compassion grows warm and tender. . . .
> I will not execute my fierce anger . . .
> for I am God and not man,
> the Holy One in your midst,
> and I will not come to destroy—
a cry that wrings the heart of every father, every parent;
a cry that brings me closer to your own heart,
you who are my heavenly Father.

As I think of my own family this night,
my parents, my children, the partner of my way,
I thank you for them, even for the pain, the anxious hours,
moments of provocation, flashes of rage and even hate.
I thank you, not because such dreadful times make possible
the good, but simply for themselves in that they are
a part of growth, of being in your world together,
of learning how to love.

One thing more:
these moments teach me about you,
and of the length and breadth and depth and height
and wonder of your bright amazing grace.
Keep me and those I love within that grace this night.

                                                    Amen.

DAY SIXTEEN
❧ ☙
Luke 1:26–38

[26]In the sixth month the angel Gabriel was sent from God to a city of Galilee named Nazareth, [27]to a virgin betrothed to a man whose name was Joseph, of the house of David; and the virgin's name was Mary. [28]And he came to her and said, "Hail, O favored one, the Lord is with you!" [29]But she was greatly troubled at the saying, and considered in her mind what sort of greeting this might be. [30]And the angel said to her, "Do not be afraid, Mary, for you have found favor with God. [31]And behold, you will conceive in your womb and bear a son, and you shall call his name Jesus.

> [32]He will be great, and will be called the Son of
> the Most High;
> and the Lord God will give to him the throne
> of his father David,
> [33]and he will reign over the house of Jacob for ever;
> and of his kingdom there will be no end."

[34]And Mary said to the angel, "How can this be, since I have no husband?" [35]And the angel said to her,

> "The Holy Spirit will come upon you,
> and the power of the Most High will overshadow you;
> therefore the child to be born will be called holy,
> the Son of God.

[36]And behold, your kinswoman Elizabeth in her old age has also conceived a son; and this is the sixth month with her who was called barren. [37]For with God nothing will be impossible." [38]And Mary said, "Behold, I am the handmaid of the Lord; let it be to me according to your word." And the angel departed from her.

Well might she have been troubled,
this innocent young peasant girl whose reverie
was broken by the mighty Gabriel himself!
> "Hail, O favored one,
>   the Lord is with you!"
is hardly the kind of greeting
one might expect to hear
while drawing water at the village well.

It is as if today, Father,
while walking with a shopping cart
along the crowded supermarket aisles
or waiting at a busy intersection
for the lights to switch from red to green,
putting in a load of laundry or picking up
the Christmas mail, I were to find myself confronted
by a being from a completely other dimension
of existence. And then that being should address
to me the news that I am favored by the Lord.

"Is this some kind of gimmick,
the bizarre prelude to a sales pitch?
What will people think? What *are* they thinking
if they can see what I am seeing at this moment?
If this is real, what am I getting into?
I'm not so sure I really want to be
the favored one of God."

Mary's response here is so typical,
her suspicion seems so natural, her question,
"What kind of greeting is this?" so understandable,
that it gives this strange, fantastic narrative
the flavor of authenticity. When I read these
troubled words of Mary, Lord, I can believe
that all this really happened.
She says just what I would have said,
and I bless her for her doubts.

Amid all the empty, wishful fantasy
that floats around this season, God,
remind me of the honesty, the integrity of Mary.
Refresh me with the genuine truth
that lies behind these ancient words.
>   Amen.

There seems to be an element
of fear involved whenever men or women
encounter the divine, whenever people are confronted
by your presence, Lord, or sense somehow
they stand on holy ground.

There is Isaiah in the temple with his cry,
    "Woe is me! For I am lost."
There is Peter in the boat on Galilee,
realizing the full identity of this One who stands
beside him in the midst of that miraculous haul of fish,
then falling to his knees and crying out,
    "Depart from me, for I am a sinful man, O Lord."
And there is Abram, Isaac, Gideon, Hannah,
all the way to John on Patmos,
that mighty host of those who knew
the shattering experience of being chosen,
called, and set apart for service;
and each one heard that firm, preliminary word
of comfort, "Do not fear. . . ."

It must truly be a fearful thing
to find oneself . . . or, rather, to be found
by you, Lord God.
The awe of the Almighty
would be sufficient, all alone,
to drive me trembling to my knees;
but in addition to all that,
there is the overwhelming fact of my own guilt,
the shabbiness and shoddiness, the vast,
pathetic emptiness that is revealed
in your pure, piercing light.

As I seek this night to recognize
the power of your presence,
as I come to realize that, if I am to find you,
I first must find myself within this dread
that all have known before you,
speak to me now your word of reassurance,
"Child, have no fear."
Then reveal to me the tasks
you would have me undertake, and equip me,
as I rest, for their accomplishing.
                    Amen.

DAY SEVENTEEN

Isaiah 61:1–4, 8–11

¹The Spirit of the Lord GOD is upon me,
  because the LORD has anointed me to bring good
    tidings to the afflicted;
  he has sent me to bind up the brokenhearted,
to proclaim liberty to the captives,
  and the opening of the prison to those who are bound;
²to proclaim the year of the LORD'S favor,
  and the day of vengeance of our God;
  to comfort all who mourn;
³to grant to those who mourn in Zion—
  to give them a garland instead of ashes,
the oil of gladness instead of mourning,
  the mantle of praise instead of a faint spirit;
that they may be called oaks of righteousness,
  the planting of the LORD, that he may be glorified.
⁴They shall build up the ancient ruins,
  they shall raise up the former devastations;
they shall repair the ruined cities,
  the devastations of many generations. . . .

⁸For I the LORD love justice,
  I hate robbery and wrong;
I will faithfully give them their recompense,
  and I will make an everlasting covenant with them.
⁹Their descendants shall be known among the nations,
  and their offspring in the midst of the peoples;
all who see them shall acknowledge them,
  that they are a people whom the LORD has blessed.

¹⁰I will greatly rejoice in the LORD,
  my soul shall exult in my God;
for he has clothed me with the garments of salvation,
  he has covered me with the robe of righteousness,
as a bridegroom decks himself with a garland,
  and as a bride adorns herself with her jewels.
¹¹For as the earth brings forth its shoots,
  and as a garden causes what is sown in it to spring up,
so the Lord GOD will cause righteousness and praise
  to spring forth before all the nations.

It is difficult to see these words
without remembering the synagogue in Nazareth,
and Jesus, as the custom was, standing up
to read them on the Sabbath day.

These were originally tidings
of great joy to Jewish exiles held captive
far from home in ancient Babylon.
The deliverance the prophet points to—
       liberty to the captives, and
       the opening of the prison—
was no metaphor, but an actual setting free,
an amnesty which sent the exiles back
to their beloved Jerusalem, where they might then
rebuild that ruined city and repair its devastation.

So many in my time still long to hear a word like this.
The world seems filled with exiles, refugees from war
or famine, politics or revenge. Every conflict
generates its own new hordes of homeless people,
doomed to live in camps and shanty towns:
Cambodians, Afghans, Vietnamese,
Palestinians and Jews, Hungarians, Poles,
East Europeans of all lands,
Ethiopians and South Africans, folk from Cuba,
Chile, El Salvador, Nicaragua, Guatemala—
people seeking justice, people fleeing justice.
This war-devastated century has known more uprooted,
homeless wanderers than any other.

The circle of my days sees little of this, Father.
If and when I move it is by choice, and to a home
at least as lovely as the one I leave behind.
I see the homeless, on my city streets,
but have little sense of those vast multitudes
who have no place to call their own.

In this season of traditional hospitality,
remind me of this presence at the gates of my own home.
Through my church, my town, my government
let me be responsive to their plight.
Anoint me with your Spirit, Lord,
to bring good news to the afflicted.
                              Amen.

I suspect we read these verses during Advent,
Father, not just because they hold great promise
of a future restoration, but also to remind us
of the purpose of this birth we look toward.
For the baby born in Bethlehem grew up,
stood up one day in his home synagogue at Nazareth,
and said that these words were fulfilled in him.

It was no easy claim to make.
He was hardly making a bid for public honor
or acclaim, the kind of speech designed to win
himself a great career of privilege and power.
In fact, the most immediate result
was that the people tried to kill him,
and two years later they succeeded.

Not only were these presumptuous claims
for a mere local carpenter, they were sacred words,
reserved over long centuries for the holy One
who was to be the goal of Israel's hope,
who was to bring fruition: full, final consummation
for all that proud, long-suffering people's yearning.
His speech was blasphemy, no less than that!
For such a crime the fate had to be death.

Therefore, as I read these ringing phrases,
I must remember, Lord my God, not just the promise
that they hold, but the price you paid to make
that promise true. I must perceive, even in Advent,
the cruel shadow of the cross and realize,
within this lovely feast, the destination set
before all time, the portent of that sword
that was to pierce Mary's soul.

The purple that the churches wear
throughout this season, Lord, returns again
in Lent. The royal cloth is also that
of passion and the spilled blood of the grape.
Now, as I kneel in wonder at the mystery
and marvel of your love made flesh
and given up for me, reveal to me
the richest depth of Christmas,
unite me with the grace that is your Son.

                                    Amen.

DAY EIGHTEEN

Philippians 4:4–9

⁴Rejoice in the Lord always; again I will say, Rejoice. ⁵Let all men know your forbearance. The Lord is at hand. ⁶Have no anxiety about anything, but in everything by prayer and supplication with thanksgiving let your requests be made known to God. ⁷And the peace of God, which passes all understanding, will keep your hearts and your minds in Christ Jesus.

⁸Finally, brethren, whatever is true, whatever is honorable, whatever is just, whatever is pure, whatever is lovely, whatever is gracious, if there is any excellence, if there is anything worthy of praise, think about these things. ⁹What you have learned and received and heard and seen in me, do; and the God of peace will be with you.

In a season so reputedly full of "joy to the world"
and "tidings of great joy," there is an uncommon dearth
of true rejoicing these pre-Christmas days, Father.
If the nightly news doesn't do it,
then the people I talk to—clerks in stores and banks,
post office workers, neighbors in the lines at
those stores and banks and post offices—
can quickly dissipate any lurking secret joy I may have
harbored for myself. It's more a weariness I sense,
a frantic busyness, almost a wish already that
this whole thing could be over with, so we could
settle down again into our worn yet comfortable ruts.
No, Lord, I don't find much rejoicing going on
around this so-called festive season.

Maybe I'm not looking in the right place.
Maybe if I tried the singles' bars, the office parties,
all those night spots and casinos where fun
is offered on the open market, maybe there is where
rejoicing can be found. But I doubt it.

Paul, of course, is much more specific about joy.
He doesn't merely say, "Cheer up! Put on a happy face!"
Paul tells me to rejoice in you, my Lord,
and that is quite a different matter.
Paul also urges me, "Rejoice always."
Not just now and then, those rare occasions when
things go my way and everything seems rosy,
but all the time, in every kind of circumstance,
he tells me to rejoice.
I am tempted to call him an empty optimist,
one of those TV merchandisers of canned cheerfulness,
till I remember what Paul lived through for the gospel
and that he wrote these very words from prison.

Paul points me to a joy that is not found here,
on the surface, but undergirds, supports, sustains
all moments of my life. This joy in you arises from
the certitude that every day, and every mood, the happy
and the sad, are in your loving hands,
hands that will bring me home at last to kneel
beside the manger. In such a joy, God,
let me spend this day.
                    Amen.

Paul seems to be given here
to all-inclusive exhortations; he has urged me
to rejoice "always," and now he says:

> In everything by prayer and supplication
> with thanksgiving let your requests
> be made known to God.

Prayer has always seemed to me to be
a unique time, Lord God, moments, even longer,
set aside from all the usual concerns, the daily bread
of work and bills, relationships and schedules,
set aside to be alone and meditative, turning all
my spiritual powers, such as they are,
toward awareness of your presence.

This "in everything" of Paul's seems to suggest
a rather different approach. Not that the quiet time,
the moments set apart, are unimportant,
rather that the other moments, the working hours,
the evenings with family and friends,
the pleasures of the garden, other hobbies,
sports and exercise, all these can be a prayer too
if practiced in your presence.

After all, Lord, you are there beside me
every instant of my day, not watching all I do
like some celestial spy; more as a companion and guide,
one who has walked this way before and knows
the pitfalls and the passing scenic splendors.
"In everything" suggests that I acknowledge
your bright radiance in the morning as I rise,
that I recognize your gift of love in loved ones
whom I greet around the table, that I give thanks
for every miracle of bread to eat, that I commit myself
into your care whenever I go forth, that I submit my work
and play to the clear vision of your truth and justice,
that I kneel to know your evening blessing
as I prepare myself for sleep.

For everything this day has seen,
with everything this night will hold,
to everything tomorrow brings, I kneel
before you now and offer thanks, in everything.

Amen.

DAY NINETEEN
❧ ❦
Jeremiah 1:4–10, 17–19

⁴Now the word of the LORD came to me saying,
⁵"Before I formed you in the womb I knew you,
and before you were born I consecrated you;
I appointed you a prophet to the nations."
⁶Then I said, "Ah, Lord GOD! Behold, I do not know how to speak, for I am only a youth." ⁷But the LORD said to me,
"Do not say, 'I am only a youth';
for to all to whom I send you you shall go,
and whatever I command you you shall speak.
⁸Be not afraid of them,
for I am with you to deliver you,
                                           says the LORD."
⁹Then the LORD put forth his hand and touched my mouth; and the LORD said to me,
"Behold, I have put my words in your mouth.
¹⁰See, I have set you this day over nations and over kingdoms,
to pluck up and to break down,
to destroy and to overthrow,
to build and to plant." . . .

¹⁷"But you, gird up your loins; arise, and say to them everything that I command you. Do not be dismayed by them, lest I dismay you before them. ¹⁸And I, behold, I make you this day a fortified city, an iron pillar, and bronze walls, against the whole land, against the kings of Judah, its princes, its priests, and the people of the land. ¹⁹They will fight against you; but they shall not prevail against you, for I am with you, says the LORD, to deliver you."

Consecrated before birth: if this was true
of Jeremiah, how much more true of the infant
born in Bethlehem's lonely barn?

This whole idea of predestination, Father,
is a thorny one for me, for many Christians.
The scriptures state quite plainly that you have
a plan for our lives; it even seems in some cases
as if certain individuals—Judas, Pharaoh, even Peter—
had little choice except to play their part in history.

On the other hand, the words of Moses
and the prophets, certainly the teachings of Jesus,
state just as clearly that your children have a choice
to make; that good or evil, life or death, cannot
be programmed in advance. Even on the question
of the incarnation of your Son, it is not clear whether
this was one last, bold attempt to save the world,
after all else—Moses, the prophets—had been rejected;
or was it planned from the beginning,
the crowning moment of a strategy
formed long before the world was given form?
As with so much of life, perhaps the answer lies
beyond the realm of either/or, within the sphere of
mystery and wonder. Certainly Job, who asked
these selfsame questions with his life, received
no clear-cut answer, was brought instead to stand
in awe before the glory of your majesty.

For me, predestination means that my own destiny,
and that of all creation, is ultimately held secure.
This belief tells me that beyond my daily choices,
beyond the long and tortuous path of human history—
its folly and its beauty—your plan
is moving steadily toward its goal.
My failures, even those of all the nations,
can set things back, delay the final harvest,
but in the end you will prevail, even as you did
in him who triumphed over death within the Easter garden.

Let that triumph be expressed in every choice I make
this day. Use me in the building of your kingdom.
                                        Amen.

Jeremiah protests here,
just as Moses did, and Amos too,
"Not me, Lord! Choose someone else.
I am no prophet, after all. Why, I cannot
even speak with confidence in public."
Yet his objection, like theirs, is overridden
by your word of courage: "Fear not! I am with you."

Your call comes through to people
in many forms within these scriptures, Lord.
Moses sees the burning bush and is drawn near.
Samuel is awakened by your voice while sleeping
in the temple, fails to recognize the call, has to be
instructed by old Eli to respond in an appropriate way.
David is called from his father's flocks upon the hills,
a young bewildered lad, to be anointed king.

And in the Gospels folk are called while fishing,
gathering taxes, riding on a mission of persecution.
So that, although we are predestined to be called by you,
the circumstances of that call,
even its content, can be highly variable.

There are those who talk as if
the only call is to the full-time ministry.
Certainly that call is an important one,
one that must be listened for and heeded,
if and when it comes. It is a formidable charge
to preach "the word of God" Sunday by Sunday
and direct it to the needs of God's own people!
But other calls are every bit as vital and may even
be more formidable. The call to raise a family,
lead a youth group, create prosperity, establish justice,
impart knowledge, feed hungry mouths, even the call
to write a book like this one: there are so many calls,
Father, and most of them, almost all, can be answered,
carried out to your glory.

You call me in this evening hour to be myself,
to see myself in your eyes, the flaws, the possibilities,
then to put myself in your hands, knowing that you
will be with me as you promised. Keep me
and my loved ones through the dark hours, Lord.

                                                    Amen.

DAY TWENTY

❧ ह ❧
James 5:7–10

⁷Be patient, therefore, brethren, until the coming of the Lord. Behold, the farmer waits for the precious fruit of the earth, being patient over it until it receives the early and the late rain. ⁸You also be patient. Establish your hearts, for the coming of the Lord is at hand. ⁹Do not grumble, brethren, against one another, that you may not be judged; behold, the Judge is standing at the doors. ¹⁰As an example of suffering and patience, brethren, take the prophets who spoke in the name of the Lord.

Christmas seems to begin a little earlier
every year. At one time, Lord—way back in
the dim and distant past of Dickens and the like—
the Christmas season really got going, I'm sure,
somewhere around the first Sunday in Advent,
and steadily progressed through days of prayer
and preparation to the great festival itself.
Nowadays, if current trends continue,
jolly old Saint Nick will soon arrive in town
just after Labor Day and riding on a dune buggy.

Patience—waiting for Christmas—
has become a lost art, Father. That measured,
steady-mounting anticipation that used to be so much
a part of this whole celebration has been abolished
in favor of instant everything, satisfaction on demand.
Yet more is lost than gained in this frantic grab
after gratification; for the deferment of excitement,
the daily drawing closer to the long looked-for moment,
was a part of the excitement in itself.

Waiting for Christmas was, still is, essential
because it compels me to deal seriously with darkness.
For all the artificial bulbs that light our wintertime,
this is still the darkest season; a time of year when
the absence of the sun evokes many other absences.
There is the absence of compassion and of justice
I pass upon the streets of every city; the absence too
of peace, object of centuries of hoping and of prayer.
As I prepare my soul for Bethlehem,
to see the darkness is as important as the light.

I once learned from an astronomer, Lord,
that to view some of the loveliest winter stars
I must rise early, well before the sun, and seek them
up against the darkest predawn sky. So with the star
of Bethlehem: its radiance can be caught only by one
prepared to face the frigid dark reality
of the world before sunrise.

Open my eyes this day, Lord God, to all the shadows
that enfold this wintered world, and my own soul,
and thus prepare me for the coming of the light.
                                                    Amen.

This patience that James urges, Lord,
is it also a patience toward you, a willingness
to wait in hope and take seriously, not just
the darkness, but also your light?

People take your light, your presence, so much
for granted nowadays—that is, if they take you at all!
The theologians, for example, are so ready to discern
your purposes, so swift to see your hands shaping
the history of our time, but always, so it seems,
in the direction they too happen to be headed.
Still others will convey the clear impression that
they have you to themselves, all sealed up inside
their large and floppy Bibles, all defined, confined
within their smug, simplistic schemes about salvation.

These four weeks of Advent waiting,
on the other hand, remind me that you are, in truth,
a mystery—a gracious mystery, but still a mystery.
The church, for all its proclamations, still exists
in a waiting world, a world where, although victory
may be assured, the consummation still lies up ahead.
We Christians are still waiting.
No matter how often or how loudly we proclaim that
we possess you and your gospel, we do not. We cannot
possess you, Lord. At the most you possess us.

Patience, waiting, seems the cruelest form
of torture for your twentieth-century servants.
Our activist souls compel us to get up and go,
to seize the bull by the horns, to strike if the iron
is even faintly warm, to slash through the Gordian knot.
Instead we are admonished to have patience, wait in hope.

"Could you not watch with me one hour?"
Your Son rebuked his disciples. Can we, can I,
not realize that the initiative is finally not mine;
that I may begin and end my Christmas season when
I please, but only you know where and when
you will be born into my life?

Teach me this truth of Advent, Lord. Let me share
the patient blessing of waiting for your Word.

                                        Amen.

DAY TWENTY-ONE
◈
Isaiah 35:1–10

¹The wilderness and the dry land shall be glad,
　the desert shall rejoice and blossom;
like the crocus ²it shall blossom abundantly,
　and rejoice with joy and singing.
The glory of Lebanon shall be given to it,
　the majesty of Carmel and Sharon.
They shall see the glory of the LORD,
　the majesty of our God.

³Strengthen the weak hands,
　and make firm the feeble knees.
⁴Say to those who are of a fearful heart,
　"Be strong, fear not!
Behold, your God
　will come with vengeance,
with the recompense of God.
　He will come and save you."

⁵Then the eyes of the blind shall be opened,
　and the ears of the deaf unstopped;
⁶then shall the lame man leap like a hart,
　and the tongue of the dumb sing for joy.
For waters shall break forth in the wilderness,
　and streams in the desert;
⁷the burning sand shall become a pool,
　and the thirsty ground springs of water;
the haunt of jackals shall become a swamp,
　the grass shall become reeds and rushes.

⁸⁻⁹And a highway shall be there,
　and it shall be called the Holy Way;
the unclean shall not pass over it, . . .
　nor shall any ravenous beast come up on it;
they shall not be found there,
　but the redeemed shall walk there.
¹⁰And the ransomed of the LORD shall return,
　and come to Zion with singing;
everlasting joy shall be upon their heads;
　they shall obtain joy and gladness,
　and sorrow and sighing shall flee away.

I love to hear these words each Advent,
their summons to participate in the glory
that you promise, Father, this vision of a desert
which rejoices, a thirsty land which sings,
a happy, blooming wilderness . . . and then
the weak hands and the feeble knees.

It helps me to feel included, Lord,
as if, in all that splendor, there will be
not just the young and strong, the fit and upright,
those still innocent and pure, but also folk like me
who feel worn around the edges, a little bit the worse
for wear, whose initial-issue equipment is beginning
to show signs of stress fatigue.

Weak hands and feeble knees: yes, Lord,
I try to keep them fit. I exercise and fight
a constant battle of the bulge, yet the enemy keeps
coming and, despite all my best efforts, the onslaught
of the years will not be turned aside.

I see others in my church and my community
whose struggle has been longer, much harder than my own,
who face unceasing pain, the terrifying breakdown of
the mind or memory, the inescapable companionship
of a disabling handicap through their remaining years,
and I marvel at their bravery, I watch as their courageous
love evokes the love of others in return, I weep for
those who never know the blessing of such grace.

The wonder of these phrases in Isaiah, the glory
of the promise you reveal in him, my Lord, is far more
than any miracle of nature—crocus in the desert,
pool sprung up in burning sand—the marvel is,
among that singing host of the redeemed who march in joy
to Zion, there is a place for my weak hands
and feeble knees, there is a song the dumb shall sing,
there is a dance for leaping by the lame.

Enlarge my vision like Isaiah's in this day,
that I recognize the promise of your grace in every life,
including mine, and—however worn, tired, or broken—
every life that I encounter on the way.

                         Amen.

Music is such a basic part
of these weeks of preparation, Father,
familiar, beloved chords and melodies
that tug, caress the heartstrings
with glad fingers of rejoicing.

There are the carols I have known
since long before I understood the glory
of their message, "Good King Wenceslas" and
"Hark! The Herald Angels," "The First Noel,"
"While Shepherds Watched," and
blessed "Silent Night."

Old Mr. Handel's miraculous *Messiah*
must be heard and joined in ringing chorus.
For me the season never really opens
till I hear the organ play those
dancing treble notes, the pacing bass,
of Johann Sebastian Bach's "Sleepers, Awake!"
while no Christmas is complete without the flute
of young Amahl, the shepherds' dance,
the entry of the kings.

Salvation Army brasses
must sound forth on the street corners
as well as the disorganized but dedicated tones
of the youth fellowships who serenade the shut-ins.
The handbell choirs send forth their pealing orisons.
Even the canned carols in the shopping malls
have their role to play throughout
this full resounding season.

And then there are
the so-called secular occasions;
The Nutcracker and *Coppélia,*
the symphonies, chorales, and chamber groups,
all vying for their moment at my ear,
their chance to move my heart.

No words can ever fully bear my thanks
to you for music and its wonder-working power.
Let my rest this night sing "Gloria in excelsis,"
and all I do tomorrow sound forth a hymn of praise.

　　　　　　　　　　　　　　　　　　Amen.

DAY TWENTY-TWO
❧ ❧
Luke 1:39–55

³⁹In those days Mary arose and went with haste into the hill country, to a city of Judah, ⁴⁰and she entered the house of Zechariah and greeted Elizabeth. ⁴¹And when Elizabeth heard the greeting of Mary, the babe leaped in her womb; and Elizabeth was filled with the Holy Spirit ⁴²and she exclaimed with a loud cry, "Blessed are you among women, and blessed is the fruit of your womb! ⁴³And why is this granted me, that the mother of my Lord should come to me? ⁴⁴For behold, when the voice of your greeting came to my ears, the babe in my womb leaped for joy. ⁴⁵And blessed is she who believed that there would be a fulfilment of what was spoken to her from the Lord." ⁴⁶And Mary said,

"My soul magnifies the Lord,
⁴⁷and my spirit rejoices in God my Savior,
⁴⁸for he has regarded the low estate of his handmaiden.
For behold, henceforth all generations will call me blessed;
⁴⁹for he who is mighty has done great things for me,
  and holy is his name.
⁵⁰And his mercy is on those who fear him
  from generation to generation.
⁵¹He has shown strength with his arm,
  he has scattered the proud in the imagination of their hearts,
⁵²he has put down the mighty from their thrones,
  and exalted those of low degree;
⁵³he has filled the hungry with good things,
  and the rich he has sent empty away.
⁵⁴He has helped his servant Israel,
  in remembrance of his mercy,
⁵⁵as he spoke to our fathers,
  to Abraham and to his posterity for ever."

I would guess, Lord God,
that most people know your presence,
sense at least a momentary touch of Holy Spirit,
at some time in their lives. But we write it off
as indigestion, or an excess of emotion.
In the cold clear light of morning we look back
and say, "How could I be so foolish?"
So we spend our days in shallows, fearful
to launch out, to entrust ourselves to mystery.

Mary was blessed, as Elizabeth points out,
because she believed; because in face of all
the skepticism, cynicism, hostile, sneering criticism
that young girl must have endured, she trusted you,
believed in what the angel told her, waited out
in patience the time of her fulfillment.

Some years ago I visited the place
where Mary heard that she would bear your Son.
It is now a crowded, overdecorated church in Nazareth,
surrounded, besieged by a host of peddlers, hawkers,
vendors: all who prey upon the tourist trade.
Once inside, I was engulfed in a great crowd,
which moved at snail's pace toward a well
behind the altar where they say the angel spoke
those strange, astounding words.

The place did not inspire me; it was crammed
with votive lamps, incense burners, ikons that seemed
grotesque to my western eye. There were even plastic covers
on the chairs and altar. I had just about decided
to opt out, to retreat into the sunshine of the street,
when a group of pilgrims somewhere in that throng
began to sing—quiet at first—"Alleluia, Alleluia."
And as that sound rose up and swelled, my heart rose up
to join it and I knew: knew the presence of a vast
and surging holiness; knew the touch, the healing,
life-renewing touch of that Living Word
which came to Mary long ago.

Lord, let me believe, if not as Mary did,
at least enough to trust what I have known in moments
such as these and build my days upon them.

                                        Amen.

If someone had been writing
Mary's speech for television, Father,
I don't think it would come out
in quite this way.

There might not be too many problems
with the first part; Mary's sheer humility
and clear integrity, while rare in our times,
should not prove too immediately offensive.
But then this girl, uneducated peasant that she is,
starts talking economics, even politics,
begins to sing about some kind of revolution
where the powerful are thrown out and the lowly,
of all people, take their places.
It is one thing, after all, to advocate
the feeding of the hungry, but when she adds to this
the idea that the rich will receive nothing,
then charity is transformed into policy,
and that will never do!

Why is it, Lord, that Christians
still insist on separating faith and politics?
Certainly the church should not take sides
in every partisan debate. But when it comes to
feeding starving people—redistributing the bounty
of your world so that children need never cry themselves
to sleep for lack of bread or basic medical supplies,
the chance to learn and grow, and make their own unique,
essential contribution to the community of life—
when it comes to issues such as these, then Christians
must speak out, even if that means involvement
in the making of political decisions.

Mary's Magnificat has been chanted,
prayed, recited by the faithful over many centuries.
Yet the transformation she proclaimed, the new priorities
she set forth for the future, have too often been
neglected, forgotten, or ignored, Father.
As these humble yet astonishing words are read
once again across your church, let them speak
with all the power of your truth,
cutting through all hocus-pocus and mystique, and calling,
calling me, to join the revolution of your Son.

                                            Amen.

DAY TWENTY-THREE
❦ ❧
Isaiah 7:10–16

[10]Again the LORD spoke to Ahaz, [11]"Ask a sign of the LORD your God; let it be deep as Sheol or high as heaven." [12]But Ahaz said, "I will not ask, and I will not put the LORD to the test." [13]And he said, "Hear then, O house of David! Is it too little for you to weary men, that you weary my God also? [14]Therefore the Lord himself will give you a sign. Behold, a young woman shall conceive and bear a son, and shall call his name Immanuel. [15]He shall eat curds and honey when he knows how to refuse the evil and choose the good. [16]For before the child knows how to refuse the evil and choose the good, the land before whose two kings you are in dread will be deserted.

After the scholars have continued their debate
about the precise meaning and translation of this word—
"young woman," "maiden," "virgin"—
after the Greek has been compared with Hebrew,
the Latin checked, the arguments for each have been
exhaustively set forth, I am left, Lord,
with the Virgin Birth, a concept, doctrine, dogma
at least as old as the New Testament, that has inspired
the deep devotion of believers from the beginning.

What does it mean; what does this revered precept
try to teach about your Son? Is it merely an attempt
to rule out sexual relations from his origin, a reflection
of the old mistaken view of sex as evil in and of itself?
Is this a way of saying that your Son was not like me,
that even from before his birth there was a basic,
essential difference that made him somehow better,
purer than I can ever hope to be?

Surely this doctrine cannot be a way
of setting Christ apart, with such a clear,
some might say unfair, advantage from the start.
If this were so, then Jesus' conquest over sin,
the whole idea of atonement, would be brought into question.
So much depends upon the statement,
"He was tempted just as we are."
Yet if his genes were somehow different, if he was not
full participant in flesh of my own flesh, bone of my
human bone, how could he bear the burden of my sin
upon the cross, be the living model I am charged to follow?

This Virgin Birth is a rich mystery to me, Lord God,
just like that other key idea of faith that he was
fully human yet, at the same time, fully God.
It suggests to me that, while Christ's birth was that of
a completely human child, it was also the miraculous,
unfathomable way you chose to join your people in their pain
and their frustration, to lead them, through the cross,
to fulfilled, abundant, everlasting life.

Teach me to grasp the meaning of this birth
for my own rebirth each day into your fuller,
truer image hidden deep within my soul.

Amen.

Of all the names and titles given to your Son
within these scriptures, Lord—Son of God,
Son of Man, Messiah, Christ, Lamb of God—
this name Immanuel conveys to me the fullest sense
of who he was and what he set out to accomplish.

The Hebrew meaning of that name—
"God with us"—contains so much in those
three monosyllables. It is a truly daring,
risky, even radical combination of ideas.
"God above us" would have seemed more proper,
surely, to express the true relationship between
humanity and the divine. "God against us"
might appear to be even more appropriate
at certain junctures in the Bible,
when your judgment and your wrath
are seen as poured out on your people.
"God before us" calls to mind the Exodus,
when you led Israel out of slavery with the fire
by night, the cloud by day. But "God with us"
sums up all of these, adds to them even more.

"God with us" tells me that the One
who reigns above the clouds, who sees and judges
all my foolishness and failings, who beckons me
to follow through the wilderness of testing
and of trial, is also to be found here at my side,
sharing the problems and the pain, tasting
those fleeting beauties, momentary ecstasies,
that sometimes brush my days with very heaven.

"God with us" signifies that when the gall
is bitter on my lips, the burden of the years
chafes rough and sore, the company with whom I had
set out has vanished and I tread, alone,
this weary path of seeking to be faithful to the past
and hopeful for the future, you are there, Lord,
you are here, beside me every step. You say to me,
"Take courage. I am with you. I have been there,
known the hurt and hollowness you feel right now,
and in my Son have conquered even death on your behalf.
Fear not, I am Immanuel—God with you."
Lord, be Immanuel for me and those I love this night.

Amen.

DAY TWENTY-FOUR

Matthew 1:18–25

[18]Now the birth of Jesus Christ took place in this way. When his mother Mary had been betrothed to Joseph, before they came together she was found to be with child of the Holy Spirit; [19]and her husband Joseph, being a just man and unwilling to put her to shame, resolved to divorce her quietly. [20]But as he considered this, behold, an angel of the Lord appeared to him in a dream, saying, "Joseph, son of David, do not fear to take Mary your wife, for that which is conceived in her is of the Holy Spirit; [21]she will bear a son, and you shall call his name Jesus, for he will save his people from their sins." [22]All this took place to fulfil what the Lord had spoken by the prophet:

[23]"Behold, a virgin shall conceive and bear a son,
and his name shall be called Emmanuel"

(which means, God with us). [24]When Joseph woke from sleep, he did as the angel of the Lord commanded him; he took his wife, [25]but knew her not until she had borne a son; and he called his name Jesus.

Joseph's role may be most difficult of all
in the events about the birth of your Son, Lord God.
His basic function is to be transparent,
scarcely there at all, a virtual nonentity.
Oh, he did his bit in getting Mary to the stable
in the first place; later he will have his part to play
in leading mother and child in flight to Egypt,
but at the birth itself Joseph fades into
the background and well-nigh disappears.

I love how Rembrandt, in his glowing
Adoration of the Shepherds, leads the eye
into a medieval barn. The scene is cast in shadows,
but the firelight picks out the kneeling shepherds there
before the crib, their staffs in hand or laid aside
on the rough floor. A boy grasps tight the collar
of a large and evil-looking dog. Mary cradles the infant
with her arm. Two women chatter in the background,
while Joseph, hair tousled, face lined, worn with fatigue,
stands, one shoulder slightly forward to protect her
from the throng, and gazes into the fire
with anxious, worried features.

There must have been an agony to being there,
just being there, in the father's place, but not, somehow,
the father; able to do nothing, say nothing that would help;
simply to stand and wonder what all this might mean for
his beloved Mary and the child that was not his.

Father, I recognize that face in Rembrandt's painting;
I know that look of anguish Joseph bears. I see it
in the news when tragedy, disaster has hit hard
and there is nothing to be done except to be there.
I see it on the faces of a family where death
has entered in and claimed a loved one from the circle
of their hearth. It is a look of blank
and helpless, stunned bewilderment.

Joseph stands for me, O God, for all who recognize
that heartache, that sense of impotence and lostness
in their lives, their families, their jobs, their world.
In Joseph's look of anguish, Lord, I find my place,
discover that I too belong beside the manger.

Amen.

Looking again tonight at Rembrandt's
Adoration of the Shepherds, Father, I discover
something more within the figure there of Joseph,
standing silent and so still. I see a light that shines
upon his worried face; I glimpse, beyond his weariness,
a new approaching wonder, a suggestion there
of slowly dawning peace—peace even for weary,
worried, fearful folk like Joseph: like me!

That stable must have been a busy place
on the first Christmas, Lord, what with birth
and all its urgencies: the shepherds, with the neighbors
they had told, all crushing in to see. Just like Advent,
really, with its hectic rush toward the deadlines—
those cards to last-minute folk I didn't expect
to get one from this year, and sort of hoped I wouldn't,
the price of postage being what it is.
And then presents to be wrapped, trees to be set up
and trimmed, parties to be given, to be gone to,
and all to be accomplished before that certain day
or it will be too late: too late to give, to welcome,
or to greet until another year, another Christmas
rolls around. And in this rush, this Christmas push
and shove, there's just no time for peace, for
standing still, for simply being there
in worry or in wonder.

Yet Joseph simply stands there.
"Don't just do something," is what he calls to me
across the centuries, into the hustle-bustle of this
frantic season, "Don't just do something, stand there!"

"Venite adoremus" sings the carol—
"O come let us adore him." It does not bid me
to obey him or to serve him, to work, strive, live,
or die for him; all that may come in your good time,
Father. But for this night, these days
that lie ahead, the call is to adore.

Teach me, Lord, to be there, simply there
as Joseph was, with nothing I can do now, nothing
to be said, nothing I can plan or even bring
except myself. Father, teach me to adore.

                              Amen.

DAY TWENTY-FIVE

Psalm 24

¹The earth is the LORD's and the fulness thereof,
   the world and those who dwell therein;
²for he has founded it upon the seas,
   and established it upon the rivers.

³Who shall ascend the hill of the LORD?
   And who shall stand in his holy place?
⁴He who has clean hands and a pure heart,
   who does not lift up his soul to what is false,
   and does not swear deceitfully.
⁵He will receive blessing from the LORD,
   and vindication from the God of his salvation.
⁶Such is the generation of those who seek him,
   who seek the face of the God of Jacob.

⁷Lift up your heads, O gates!
   and be lifted up, O ancient doors!
   that the King of glory may come in.
⁸Who is the King of glory?
   The LORD, strong and mighty,
   the LORD, mighty in battle!
⁹Lift up your heads, O gates!
   and be lifted up, O ancient doors!
   that the King of glory may come in.
¹⁰Who is this King of glory?
   The LORD of hosts,
   he is the King of glory!

Clean hands and a pure heart
as the prerequisite for blessing,
as the entrance qualification
to stand in your holy place,
would rule out most Christians I know, Lord,
and would certainly exclude me.

This ancient entrance rite
into the temple in Jerusalem
with its stately question and response
is a lovely thing, a song of elegant beauty,
but its message, with that high and lofty tone
of holiness, sets standards which, in honesty,
few if any of your servants could hope to meet.
Who is there who can say his hands are clean?
Who is she who can go even further
and offer up a pure heart?

As I review these strict demands
I am reminded of the Sermon on the Mount,
where Jesus took the teachings of the Jewish law
and made them even more impossible to attain, saying,
"You have heard it said . . . but I say unto you. . . ."
Jesus radicalized those ancient laws, refocusing
their judgment on the heart, the workings of the mind
and the imagination, not merely the specific outward
acts that I commit, or fail to carry out.

Perhaps we read this psalm in Advent, Father,
as a reminder that, in terms of the law, we were,
still are, completely bankrupt in your sight.
These stringent words remind me,
even as they judge me, that in the fullness
of your time, One did appear, One who
        has clean hands and a pure heart,
        who does not lift up his soul to what is false,
        and does not swear deceitfully.
and it is his appearing, and the promise of salvation
that he brings—as in his purity he enters your temple
and flings wide its doors to all—that I commemorate
and celebrate in these December days.

Send me forth into this day, Lord, in his purity.

                                        Amen.

These are majestic words, Lord God,
an antiphon that must have sounded and resounded
about the temple as the folk of ancient Israel
proclaimed the entrance of their God and King.
There is a note of triumph in these questions
and their answers that almost lets me hear
the temple trumpets in full cry.
I can see in my mind's eye those temple gates
closed tight, the throng without, the echoing throng
within; and then the shout of holy exultation as
the barriers come down, the portals yield,
the heavy doors swing open to welcome
and to hail the Lord of hosts.

I love to hear this psalm sung or chanted
in this awe-inspiring way by choir and congregation
in the worship of these looking-forward days.

Yet, for all the grandeur, pomp, and circumstance
of this ceremonial setting, there is a miracle,
the miracle of Christmas, at work within these words.
Behind these festive shouts there lies a paradox,
a paradox that exists at the heart of this faith
of mine, O God. And that paradox is this:
that the Almighty One, the Supreme, Omniscient,
Omnipotent, and Omnipresent God—the power that is
so far beyond my comprehension that any word
I might use to speak of it is false of necessity—
that this power, so lifted up and so remote,
draws near, comes close to me, and enters
into the very place I dwell.

In this mighty psalm of entrance
it is possible to see the babe of Bethlehem,
to glimpse, about his unpretentious birth, the panoply
of angels and archangels that the artists clearly saw,
all gathered there and singing, "Glory!
Glory to God in the highest. And on earth, peace."

Grant me, Lord, a new appreciation of the cosmic
scope of all that I commemorate in this feast.
With the simplicity of faith, let me also know
the grandeur of this hour of holy triumph.
                                        Amen.

DAY TWENTY-SIX
❧ ❦
John 19:25b–27

[25]. . . But standing by the cross of Jesus were his mother, and his mother's sister, Mary the wife of Clopas, and Mary Magdalene. [26]When Jesus saw his mother, and the disciple whom he loved standing near, he said to his mother, "Woman, behold, your son!" [27]Then he said to the disciple, "Behold, your mother!" And from that hour the disciple took her to his own home.

There must be some mistake, Lord.
This reading from Saint John belongs in Holy Week,
not Advent. What is the point? Why should I be reading
about Jesus on the cross already, when I am busy
preparing to celebrate his birth?
First things first, after all;
this touching farewell scene between Jesus
and his grieving mother will soon have its proper turn
as Lent and springtime move me toward Easter.

Yet the lectionary makers
must have had their own good reasons
for suggesting this particular selection.
Could it be that their intent is to counteract
the perennial tendency to sentimentalize the manger birth—
the sugar-sweetness of those precious illustrations
on the Christmas cards—by employing a device
like those fast-forward scenes
I sometimes see in movies, thus
reminding readers of the shocking outcome
of this "charming" little narrative?

This final scene at Calvary
may be especially well chosen in that as Mary,
at the outset, gives love's gift of life to her child,
so Jesus, here at the end, gives his dying gift
of love back to his mother. He entrusts her
to the care of one he loves; likewise
he commits this loved disciple to Mary's care.

One might see these words as Jesus' last bequest:
The final will and testament of Jesus bar Joseph—
Jesus of Nazareth—sometime carpenter, preacher,
healer, redeemer, the Christ.
"Having no worldly goods left to bestow,
I take this one gift I do have,
the living love of God so deep within me,
and I bestow it on you, Mother, and on you,
my friend. Behold your son! Behold your mother!"

Grant me, Lord, a genuine rejoicing in this season's grace
and loveliness, yet keep my eyes clear on the goal,
the end to which this child was born.
                                        Amen.

Jesus, in these dying words, stripped
of every possession, the very clothing he had worn,
disposes now the only thing they left to him,
his mother's love, and that of his closest disciple
and dear friend. And in these poignant phrases,
he gives them to each other: "Behold your son! . . .
Behold your mother!"

In this season, Lord, of splendid, even
sacrificial giving, it is good to be reminded of this,
the very last gift Jesus gave. Through his birth
and sacrificial death upon the cross, Jesus gives us
to each other; I mean your people, Lord.
He sets us free from all the selfish and protective fears
that bind us to ourselves, free to recognize that other,
deeper, truer "tie that binds," the bond of human love.

I can still recall with wonder
the first time I held a life, the life
of my own child, within my arms—the glad relief,
the inexpressible joy, the humbling sense of privilege
in all you had entrusted to my care. That gratitude
and tenderness that flowed so freely from me then
has been set free for all through this
rich gift that Jesus brings.

Jesus gives us to each other,
entrusts me to my neighbor, entrusts my neighbor
to my care. And of all the gifts that I receive,
not just for Christmas, but each day—
the gifts of health, abilities, and skills,
of education, heritage, and nation, the many freedoms
I so often take for granted—the most valuable,
most precious gift you pour out for me every day
is this gift of other people: sisters, brothers,
comrades for the journey, those with whom to share
this glorious thing called love, which cannot be
unless it be together, given and received with
all our fellow children, Father.

In this season of the family, remind me of
that wider, richer family that Jesus came to give to me.
Then show me how to be your gift to all I meet.
Amen.

DAY TWENTY-SEVEN
Micah 5:2–5a

²But you, O Bethlehem Ephrathah,
  who are little to be among the clans of Judah,
from you shall come forth for me
  one who is to be ruler in Israel,
whose origin is from of old,
  from ancient days.
³Therefore he shall give them up until the time
  when she who is in travail has brought forth;
then the rest of his brethren shall return
  to the people of Israel.
⁴And he shall stand and feed his flock in the strength of the LORD,
  in the majesty of the name of the LORD his God.
And they shall dwell secure, for now he shall be great
  to the ends of the earth.
⁵And this shall be peace.

What a surprise for Herod,
and for all the big wheels ever since,
to discover this quiet prophecy from Micah
that the hope of all the yearning world shall come
from tiny, obscure Bethlehem, a hick town in Ephrathah,
the family home of Ruth's first husband
and of Jesse, David's father.

Is there a sign right here, Lord,
not only to the birthplace of Messiah
but also of encouragement to all who are obscure,
unknown, who seem unlikely ever to make
much difference in the world?

This word reminds me
of the way you chose your leaders
in those days of old. For Moses was a hunted man,
a fearful refugee in hiding in the wilderness.
Gideon was an unknown farmer's son, and the host
he led to battle in your name was minuscule,
almost laughable in military terms.
Saul, when he was chosen king, was chosen
out of Benjamin, the smallest tribe in Israel,
and David was the youngest of his father's sons,
so unregarded he was not invited home to stand
before old Samuel in his quest for a new king.
Do you specialize in the unlikely, Father?
Even Israel herself was just a motley band of slaves
when you picked them up and led them out to be
your chosen people, a beacon for the rest of us to follow.

How marvelous that in these days of show
and splash and clout, when everyone wants everyone
to think they are more famous, more rich
and influential than they really are, you come
among us as a peasant child of unsure parentage,
hailing from the kind of town no one would ever claim
to have been born in, even visited, before that time.

Teach me that in your sight what may appear
insignificant is actually vital, that everything I do
or say might provide room in which your living word
of grace can be reborn into this needy world.
                                        Amen.

116   *A CHILD IS BORN*

This image of the One who is to come portrayed
as shepherd, Lord, pervades the ancient prophecies,
is filled, for me, with power and deep emotion.
Handel, in his *Messiah*, sets Isaiah's version
of these words to some of the most satisfying—
both comforting and soul-inspiring—
music I have ever heard.

The warm embracing tones
of the contralto pour out the gentleness
and nurturing, firm assurance of the text,
then the bright, shimmering soprano
snatches up the words and melody,
repeats them in a higher register,
conveying all the soaring, shining, starlike promise,
the inspiration and encouragement for the road ahead,
that is also offered to the soul within
this tender-cherished picture of a shepherd
with his beloved flock.

Father, there is guidance promised here
and sure protection, provision also
for the journey, the strong assurance
that, whatever it may be that lies ahead,
your steadfast hand will lead me,
your everlasting arms will be about me,
the sure refuge of your evening benediction
will, in the end, enfold me.

As I draw close to the ending
of another busy day; as I draw closer
to the holiday, the holy day itself,
when all my frenzied plans and preparations
will have to be complete;
as I draw closer also to that day
of which I prefer not to think, that day
when everything will be, for me, completed—
for better or for worse—fill my mind,
feed my soul with this blessed image
of the faithful shepherd and his flock.

This night, may I lie down and rest
in pastures green, beside still waters.

                    Amen.

DAY TWENTY-EIGHT
❧ ❧
Romans 16:25–27

[25]Now to him who is able to strengthen you according to my gospel and the preaching of Jesus Christ, according to the revelation of the mystery which was kept secret for long ages [26]but is now disclosed and through the prophetic writings is made known to all nations, according to the command of the eternal God, to bring about the obedience of faith—[27]to the only wise God be glory for evermore through Jesus Christ! Amen.

So this is what the mystics
and the prophets all looked forward to.
This is what philosophers and scientists,
sculptors, painters, singers, poets had all been
struggling with and striving to express.
Here is the answer to those riddles, myths,
and legends of the ancient world:
a newborn baby in a manger.

It seems absurd, on the face of it, Father;
it must have struck some people as a joke
that, instead of some arcane and complex formula,
some axiom encapsuling the wisdom of the ages,
or even some deliverer—a golden hero on
a milk-white steed—you sent a child,
this infant born in Bethlehem.

Yet there is mystery revealed
in every infant born into this world:
the mystery by which a child can reach out,
touch, and seize the heart, can win its way around
long years of thick-encrusted selfishness
and callousness, and gentle folk into affection,
even compassion once again.

There is the mystery through which a child
can demand what it wills of us and never be refused.
A conquering hero might demand my vote, my voice,
my money, even my strong right arm, and receive it
for a time. But every child demands a lifetime,
or at least my undivided love and nurture for some
twenty years and more, and gets it with a smile.

And then, the greatest mystery of all,
there is redemption in a child. This tiny
helpless babe can melt a heart and turn a life around,
transform a miserable skinflint like old Scrooge
into a second father to young Tiny Tim; can take my life,
ease open its thick protective shell, and seed a pearl
to gleam with all the luster of your love, my God.

Unveil your mystery to me this day, Lord God,
let it redeem me into life poured out in love.

                                        Amen.

"Gloria in excelsis Deo!"
was what the angels sang as
the glory of the Lord shone round
about those humble, startled shepherds.

And old Simeon at the temple in Jerusalem
witnessed to that same glory in his song—
the Nunc Dimittis—as he took your Son
into his trembling arms and blessed you, Lord,
that he had lived to see the day.

John testified that
            we have beheld his glory, glory as
            of the only Son from the Father.
And Paul sees glory, glory for evermore!

What is this "glory," Father, that pervades
not just the story of your Son but psalms and prophecy,
epistles, the whole content of this book of books?
How can I define the meaning of this term,
make sense of it, not just to others
but also to myself?

It strikes me, Lord, that glory
cannot be defined, can only be experienced
and then spoken of in terms of that experience.
Glory, then, has much in common with that feeling
that I knew the first Christmas I remember as I crept
downstairs before the dawn and felt my fingers meet,
explore, a filled-to-bursting Christmas stocking
hanging plump below the stairway banister.

I must have brushed with glory coming home on leave
one Christmas Eve as, waiting for a train and wandering
late and far along the frosty station platform,
I was captured by the splendor of the star-encrusted sky
and stood long in conversation with that other star
and three other weary travelers long ago.

In the days ahead, good Lord, let me find glory
in my parents' eyes, my children's laughter, the quiet,
thankful glance of the one with whom I share my days,
and even in the hoping of my own enchanted heart
                                    Amen.

CHRISTMAS EVE
ﻋﺞ ﻫﻮ
Isaiah 60:1–6

¹Arise, shine; for your light has come,
  and the glory of the LORD has risen upon you.
²For behold, darkness shall cover the earth,
  and thick darkness the peoples;
but the LORD will arise upon you,
  and his glory will be seen upon you.
³And nations shall come to your light,
  and kings to the brightness of your rising.

⁴Lift up your eyes round about, and see;
  they all gather together, they come to you;
your sons shall come from far,
  and your daughters shall be carried in the arms.
⁵Then you shall see and be radiant,
  your heart shall thrill and rejoice;
because the abundance of the sea shall be turned to you,
  the wealth of the nations shall come to you.
⁶A multitude of camels shall cover you,
  the young camels of Midian and Ephah;
  all those from Sheba shall come.
They shall bring gold and frankincense,
  and shall proclaim the praise of the LORD.

Properly, of course, the three Wise Men
should have to wait until Epiphany—
the twelfth day of Christmas—according to
the official schedules of the liturgical year.
Unofficially, of course, in the minds of the people,
the whole sequence of events has been compressed,
and so the Magi are right there, in manger scenes,
on greeting cards, standing holding gifts
next to the shepherds.

I'm glad to have this reading from Isaiah
here on Christmas Eve, not just because it lifts up
once again my opening theme of light in darkness,
but also, Lord, because this prophecy—where
the wealth of nations, camels, and folk from Sheba
are all mentioned beside gold and frankincense—
cannot but conjure up for me the story of the kings.

So much has been imagined, Lord, so many details
to fill out the visit of Matthew's Wise Men from the east.
The Gospel does not even give the number three,
and yet they have so captivated the imagination
that whole books, poems, and plays have been composed
around their quest. It is partly the exotic, I suppose,
that fascinates; the idea of kings on camels—
astrologers with names like Caspar, Melchior, Balthazar—
arriving to pay homage at this hasty, humble birth.

But more than the exotic is found here.
The wisdom of the world is brought to kneel
and join with simple countryfolk in adoration.
The nations of the world—"Gentiles," the Jews
would call them—are represented in these royal figures.
The offerings they bring, gold, frankincense,
mysterious myrrh, foreshadow all the gifts that are
so much a part of how we celebrate today, Lord God.
Their outwitting of King Herod shows, right at the start,
the shadow that will later fall across your Son,
and hints at his deliverance.

Lord, I thank you for the lessons of the Magi
and pray that I might add my gift to theirs,
the gift of simple and sincere devotion.
                                        Amen.

CHRISTMAS EVE

Luke 2:1–20

¹In those days a decree went out from Caesar Augustus that all the world should be enrolled. ²This was the first enrollment, when Quirinius was governor of Syria. ³And all went to be enrolled, each to his own city. ⁴And Joseph also went up from Galilee, from the city of Nazareth, to Judea, to the city of David, which is called Bethlehem, because he was of the house and lineage of David, ⁵to be enrolled with Mary, his betrothed, who was with child. ⁶And while they were there, the time came for her to be delivered. ⁷And she gave birth to her first-born son and wrapped him in swaddling cloths, and laid him in a manger, because there was no place for them in the inn.

⁸And in that region there were shepherds out in the field, keeping watch over their flock by night. ⁹And an angel of the Lord appeared to them, and the glory of the Lord shone around them, and they were filled with fear. ¹⁰And the angel said to them, "Be not afraid; for behold, I bring you good news of a great joy which will come to all the people; ¹¹for to you is born this day in the city of David a Savior, who is Christ the Lord. ¹²And this will be a sign for you: you will find a babe wrapped in swaddling cloths and lying in a manger." ¹³And suddenly there was with the angel a multitude of the heavenly host praising God and saying,

¹⁴"Glory to God in the highest,
   and on earth peace among men with
   whom he is pleased!"

¹⁵When the angels went away from them into heaven, the shepherds said to one another, "Let us go over to Bethlehem and see this thing that has happened, which the Lord has made known to us." ¹⁶And they went with haste, and found Mary and Joseph, and the babe lying in a manger. ¹⁷And when they saw it they made known the saying which had been told them concerning this child; ¹⁸and all who heard it wondered at what the shepherds told them. ¹⁹But Mary kept all these things, pondering them in her heart. ²⁰And the shepherds returned, glorifying and praising God for all they had heard and seen, as it had been told them.

For all the marvel of these blessed,
cherished, and well-rounded verses of Saint Luke;
for all the magic that I never fail to feel
when I hear them read aloud in church this very eve;
they tell, at least until the angels come upon the scene,
of totally mundane and commonplace events.

New taxes may be newsworthy, but they are hardly
information one would hand down over centuries.
A weary couple traveling far from home
because of government regulations,
even an expectant girl without a place to lay her head,
these are not the stuff one might expect
to find immortalized. And this birthing of
a first-born son, the wrapping him in covers,
the laying of him in a feed box for a bed:
this happens every second of my birth-exploding century,
has happened since the birth of time itself.

Death and taxes, birth and taxes,
things one can be sure of, can rely on
to endure upon this human scene as long
as there is a human scene left to endure.
Why do we make such a fuss about it all, Father?
What is there in these everyday events
to justify their annual remembering,
rehearsal, repetition?

Might it be that
in the very ordinariness of your Son's birth
there lies the first disclosure of his message,
of the great good news? Might it be, this very night,
that you are telling me to look for meaning,
mystery, and miracle right here inside
the matter-of-fact problems, pains, potentials
that make up the daily round?

I pray this may be so, Lord God,
because the miracle of Christmas that I need
will not be found in far-off Bethlehem,
or even on the decorated altar of the church,
but in the birth of hope and trust and love
deep in my ordinary heart.
                              Amen.

CHRISTMAS DAY
Isaiah 52:1–2, 7–10

¹Awake, awake,
   put on your strength, O Zion;
put on your beautiful garments,
   O Jerusalem, the holy city;
for there shall no more come into you
   the uncircumcised and the unclean.
²Shake yourself from the dust, arise,
   O captive Jerusalem;
loose the bonds from your neck,
   O captive daughter of Zion. . . .

⁷How beautiful upon the mountains
   are the feet of him who brings good tidings,
who publishes peace, who brings good tidings of good,
   who publishes salvation,
   who says to Zion, "Your God reigns."
⁸Hark, your watchmen lift up their voice,
   together they sing for joy;
for eye to eye they see
   the return of the LORD to Zion.
⁹Break forth together into singing,
   you waste places of Jerusalem;
for the LORD has comforted his people,
   he has redeemed Jerusalem.
¹⁰The LORD has bared his holy arm
   befefore the eyes of all the nations;
and all the ends of the earth shall see
   the salvation of our God.

What a day, what a morning of awakenings, Lord!
Of all the mornings of the year, those dreary dawning
hours when it takes the full combined endeavors
of the will plus the alarm clock to raise me
from the pillow, then an even more colossal effort
to rouse the kids for school; after all of those
bedraggled, yawning, groaning scenes around
the breakfast table, this day is a veritable miracle!

The children leap from bed before the sun
has ventured near the winter skyline. Parents
scurry round in the pitch dark to see that cameras
are loaded, hidden tape recorders switched on.
And then the glorious moment when the tree is lit,
and one and all can view the vast array of parcels,
packages, bundles, bulging stockings, before settling
down to hours of suspense, then swift surprise,
squealed delight, and thankful hugs.

It would be easy, Lord, to criticize all this:
the waste, the trash, the sad attempt to buy affection
in a splash of wild extravagance. Yet, for all of that,
this is a genuine time of family and fun; a day when
games are played together, books are read and puzzles
puzzled, a meal is eaten family-style, smiles
and kisses are in plentiful supply; a day
when memories are brought forth, dusted off,
and handed round, favorite old family stories find
themselves retold, and toasts are drunk, prayers are said,
hands are held, and promises are made and even kept.

Is there, might there be in all of this,
at least an inkling of the beauty and the hope
that old Isaiah sang about? May I find in moments
such as these an echo of those "tidings of great joy"?
I wonder, would the Christ-child, if he sat beneath our
sparkling tree, condemn as crass and empty all he saw?
Or might he laugh and cheer and clap his sticky hands
with glee to see his miracle take place again
and life become abundant shared in love?

Make this bright day complete now
with the greatest gift, your presence, Lord.
                                        Amen.

CHRISTMAS DAY

John 1:1–14

[1]In the beginning was the Word, and the Word was with God, and the Word was God. [2]He was in the beginning with God; [3]all things were made through him, and without him was not anything made that was made. [4]In him was life, and the life was the light of men. [5]The light shines in the darkness, and the darkness has not overcome it.

[6]There was a man sent from God, whose name was John. [7]He came for testimony, to bear witness to the light, that all might believe through him. [8]He was not the light, but came to bear witness to the light.

[9]The true light that enlightens every man was coming into the world. [10]He was in the world, and the world was made through him, yet the world knew him not. [11]He came to his own home, and his own people received him not. [12]But to all who received him, who believed in his name, he gave power to become children of God; [13]who were born, not of blood nor of the will of the flesh nor of the will of man, but of God.

[14]And the Word became flesh and dwelt among us, full of grace and truth; we have beheld his glory, glory as of the only Son from the Father.

After Luke's beloved narrative—
Mary, Joseph, the baby wrapped in swaddling clothes,
and those shepherds from the hillsides around Bethlehem—
after Matthew's warning angels and the Magi
with their gifts, their outwitting of King Herod,
it comes as a surprise, even a shock, Father,
to find this Christmas story of Saint John
spelled out in such a different way.

He begins, "In the beginning, . . ."
leading my contemplation back to those
first words of Genesis, suggesting to me that
what follows is a new creation, yet one in which
that same creative power, your own Word, Lord God,
takes shape again as the expression of your love.
He speaks of life, of light that shines in darkness,
of One who came to his own family, his own home,
yet was turned away, rejected.
John also tells of those who did receive him,
who believed in who he was and what he stood for,
and in believing were reborn to become part
of this your new creation, sisters, brothers,
in a re-created family of humankind.

It strikes me, Lord, that this story,
John's version of what happened there at Bethlehem,
is essential to the meaning of those narratives
the other writers told. John here fills in
the background, adds depth and height,
the full dimension of eternity, to the simple charm
and wonder that I find in Luke and Matthew.
My faith would be a poorer, plainer thing
without those lovely scenes about the manger,
but without these profound words of John, who sets
all that occurred within the total context of your grace,
my Christmas would, too easily, dissolve into
a pretty picture or a sentimental tale.

As I reread these rich, transcendent words,
renew my awe, Lord God, before the magnitude
and mystery of Christmas, help me kneel in silent wonder
as the secret of the ages, of the universe, is revealed
within the human cry of a newborn child.
                                        Amen.